At Sylvan, we believe that a lifelong love of learning begins at an early age, and we are glad you have chosen our resources to help your children experience the joy of mathematics as they build critical reasoning skills. We know that the time you spend with your children reinforcing the lessons learned in school will contribute to their love of learning.

Success in math requires more than just memorizing basic facts and algorithms; it also requires children to make sense of size, shape, and numbers as they appear in the world. Children who can connect their understanding of math to the world around them will be ready for the challenges of mathematics as they advance to more complex topics.

We use a research-based, step-by-step process in teaching math at Sylvan that includes thought-provoking math problems and activities. As students increase their success as problem solvers, they become more confident. With increasing confidence, students build even more success. The design of the Sylvan workbooks will help you to help your children build the skills and confidence that will contribute to success in school.

We're excited to partner with you to support the development of confident, well-prepared independent learners!

The Sylvan Team

Sylvan Learning Center
Unleash your child's potential here

No matter how big or small the academic challenge, every child has the ability to learn. But sometimes children need help making it happen. Sylvan believes every child has the potential to do great things. And we know better than anyone else how to tap into that academic potential so that a child's future really is full of possibilities. Sylvan Learning Center is the place where your child can build and master the learning skills needed to succeed and unlock the potential you know is there.

The proven, personalized approach of our in-center programs deliver unparalleled results that other supplemental education services simply can't match. Your child's achievements will be seen not only in test scores and report cards but outside the classroom as well. And when he starts achieving his full potential, everyone will know it. You will see a new level of confidence come through in everything he does and every interaction he has.

How can Sylvan's personalized in-center approach help your child unleash his potential?

- Starting with our exclusive Sylvan Skills Assessment®, we pinpoint your child's exact academic needs.

- Then we develop a customized learning plan designed to achieve your child's academic goals.

- Through our method of skill mastery, your child will not only learn and master every skill in his personalized plan, he will be truly motivated and inspired to achieve his full potential.

To get started, simply contact your local Sylvan Learning Center to set up an appointment. And to learn more about Sylvan and our innovative in-center programs, call 1-800-EDUCATE or visit www.SylvanLearning.com. *With over 850 locations in North America, there is a Sylvan Learning Center near you!*

2nd Grade
Jumbo Math Success
Workbook

Published in the United States by Random House, Inc., New York, and in Canada by Random House of Canada Limited, Toronto.

This book was previously published with the title *2nd Grade Super Math Success* as a trade paperback by Sylvan Learning, Inc., an imprint of Penguin Random House LLC, in 2010.

www.sylvanlearning.com

Created by Smarterville Productions LLC
Producer & Editorial Direction: The Linguistic Edge
Producer: TJ Trochlil McGreevy
Writer: Amy Kraft
Cover and Interior Illustrations: Shawn Finley, Tim Goldman, and Duendes del Sur
Layout and Art Direction: SunDried Penguin
Director of Product Development: Russell Ginns

First Edition

ISBN: 978-0-375-43050-3

This book is available at special discounts for bulk purchases for sales promotions or premiums. For more information, write to Special Markets/Premium Sales, 1745 Broadway, MD 6-2, New York, New York 10019 or e-mail specialmarkets@randomhouse.com.

PRINTED IN THE UNITED STATES

Basic Math Success Contents

Math Games & Puzzles Contents

Math in Action Contents

2nd Grade
Basic Math Success

Get in Place

WRITE how many tens and ones you see. Then WRITE the number they make.

1.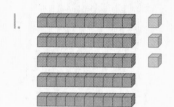

Tens	Ones
5	3
= **53**

2.

Tens	Ones
2	5
= 25

3.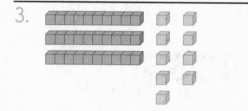

Tens	Ones
3	9
= 39

4.

Tens	Ones
1	7
= 17

5.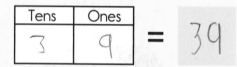

Tens	Ones
7	2
= 72

6.

Tens	Ones
8	1
= 81

7.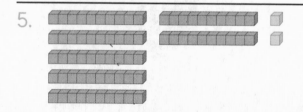

Tens	Ones
4	6
= 46

8.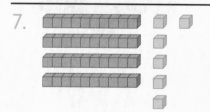

Tens	Ones
6	8
= 68

Get in Place

 = 10¢ = 1¢

WRITE how many tens and ones you see.
Then WRITE the number they make.

1.

Tens	Ones
1	6

= 16

2.

Tens	Ones
4	9

= 49

3.

Tens	Ones
8	3

= 83

4.

Tens	Ones
7	5

= 75

5.

Tens	Ones
5	8

= 58

6.

Tens	Ones
3	2

= 32

7.

Tens	Ones
9	4

= 94

8.

Tens	Ones
6	7

= 67

Place Value

Get in Place

WRITE how many hundreds, tens, and ones you see. Then WRITE the number they make.

1.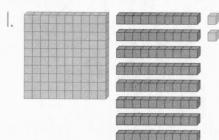

Hundreds	Tens	Ones
1	8	2

= 182

2.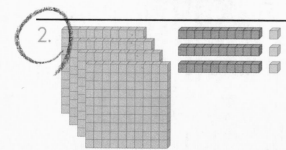

Hundreds	Tens	Ones
4	3	3

= 433

3.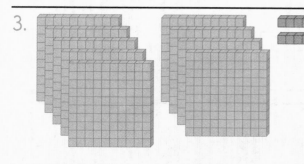

Hundreds	Tens	Ones
9	2	5

= 925

4.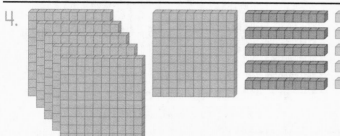

Hundreds	Tens	Ones
6	5	7

= 657

5.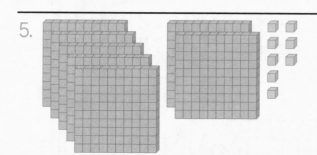

Hundreds	Tens	Ones
7	0	8

= 708

Number Match

CIRCLE the picture in each row that matches the number.

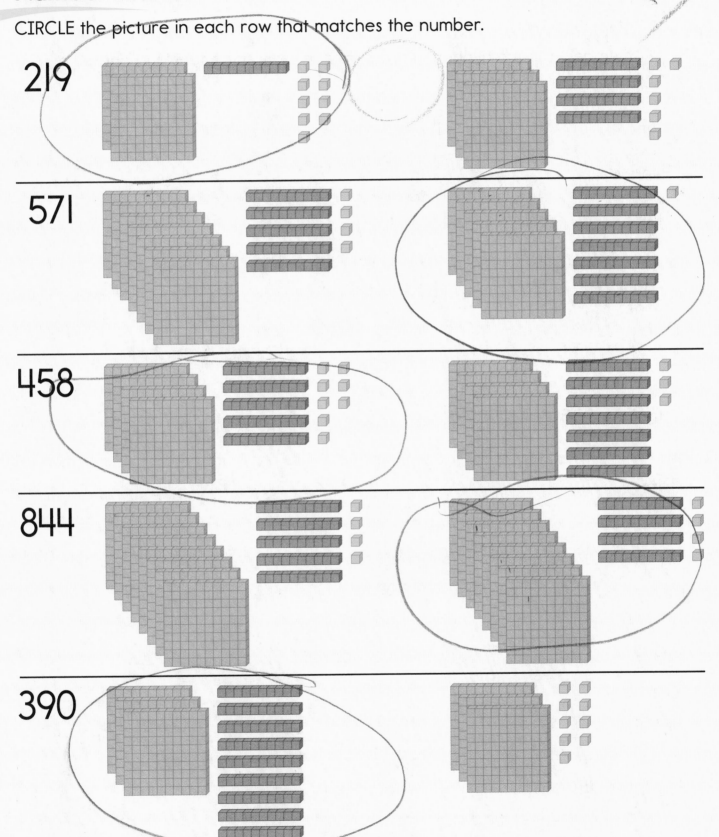

219

571

458

844

390

Place Value

Write the Number

WRITE the number words.

HINT: Remember to put a hyphen in numbers connecting the tens and ones, like seventy-four or thirty-three.

1 one	11 eleven	30 thirty
2 two	12 twelve	40 forty
3 three	13 thirteen	50 fifty
4 four	14 fourteen	60 sixty
5 five	15 fifteen	70 seventy
6 six	16 sixteen	80 eighty
7 seven	17 seventeen	90 ninety
8 eight	18 eighteen	100 one hundred
9 nine	19 nineteen	
10 ten	20 twenty	

1. 162   one hundred sixty-two

2. 374   three hundred seventy four

3. 250   two hundred fifty

4. 816   eight hundred sixteen

5. 643   six hundred forty three

6. 495   four hundred ninty five

Match Up

DRAW lines to connect the numbers and words that go together.

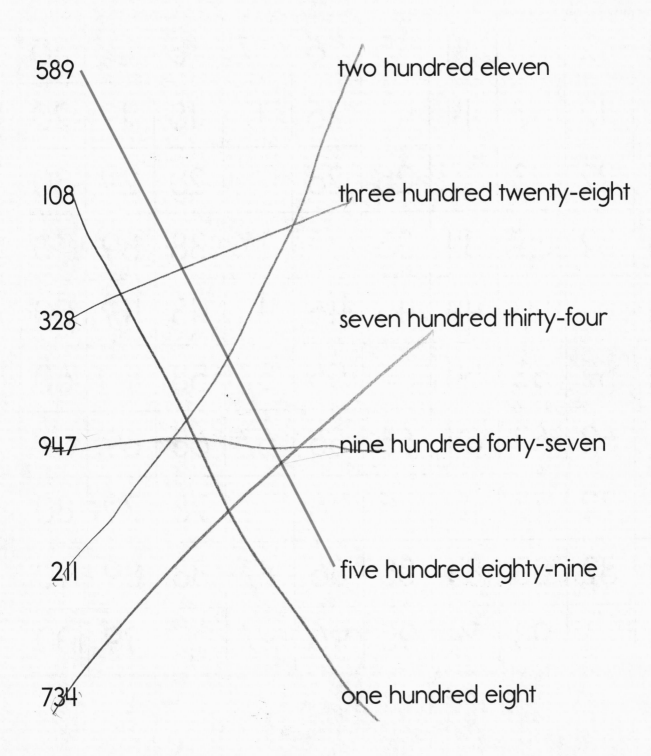

589

108

328

947

211

734

two hundred eleven

three hundred twenty-eight

seven hundred thirty-four

nine hundred forty-seven

five hundred eighty-nine

one hundred eight

Holey Hundreds!

WRITE the missing numbers on the chart. Then COLOR the chart by following the directions on the next page.

1	2	3	4	5	6	7	8	9	10
11	12	13	14	15	16	17	18	19	20
21	22	23	24	25	26	27	28	29	30
31	32	33	34	35	36	37	38	39	40
41	42	43	44	45	46	47	48	49	50
51	52	53	54	55	56	57	58	59	60
61	62	63	64	65	66	67	68	69	70
71	72	73	74	75	76	77	78	79	80
81	82	83	84	85	86	87	88	89	90
91	92	93	94	95	96	97	98	99	100

1. COLOR number 33 blue.
2. COLOR number 57 red.
3. COLOR number 94 purple.
4. COLOR number 52 orange.

5. COLOR the number that is 2 more than 7 blue.
6. COLOR the number that is 8 more than 17 red.
7. COLOR the number that is 10 less than 71 purple.
8. COLOR the number that is 16 less than 56 orange.

9. Starting at number 8, SKIP COUNT by 10 and COLOR the squares yellow.
10. Starting at number 75, SKIP COUNT by 5 and COLOR the squares green.

1	2		4	5	6	7	8		10
	12	13	14		16	17	18	19	20
21	22	23		25	26		28	29	30
31	37		34	35		37	38	39	40
41		43	44	45	46	47	48	49	50
51		53	54		56	57	58		60
	62	63	64	65	66	67	68	69	
71	72	73		75	76		78	79	80
81	82	83	84	85	86	87	88	89	90
91		93	94	95	96	97		99	100

Pattern Patch

WRITE the missing numbers in the boxes.

| 82 | 83 | 84 | | 86 | 87 | | 89 |

| 103 | | | 106 | 107 | | 109 | |

| | 344 | 345 | | 347 | | | 350 |

| 719 | 720 | | | | | | |

| 566 | | | | | | | 573 |

| | | | | | | 856 | 857 |

2

Get in Line

WRITE the missing numbers on each number line.

234 235 236 237 ⬚ 239 240 ⬚

⬚ 982 983 ⬚ ⬚ 986 ⬚ 988

97 ⬚ ⬚ ⬚ 101 ⬚ 103 ⬚

874 875 ⬚ ⬚ ⬚ ⬚ ⬚ ⬚

699 ⬚ ⬚ ⬚ ⬚ ⬚ ⬚ 706

⬚ ⬚ ⬚ ⬚ ⬚ ⬚ 401 402

Get in Line

SKIP COUNT and WRITE the missing numbers on each number line.

Skip count by 2:

+2

2   4   6   8

Skip count by 5:

50   55   60

Skip count by 10:

60   70   80

Skip count by 3:

15   18   21

Skip count by 8:

8   16   24

Skip count by 6:

42   48   54

②

Pattern Patch

DETERMINE what number is being used for skip counting. Then WRITE the rest of the pattern.

66	68	70					

20	30	40					

15	20	25					

27	30	33					

62	66	70					

42	49	56					

Which One?

CIRCLE the picture in each pair that has **more** than the other.

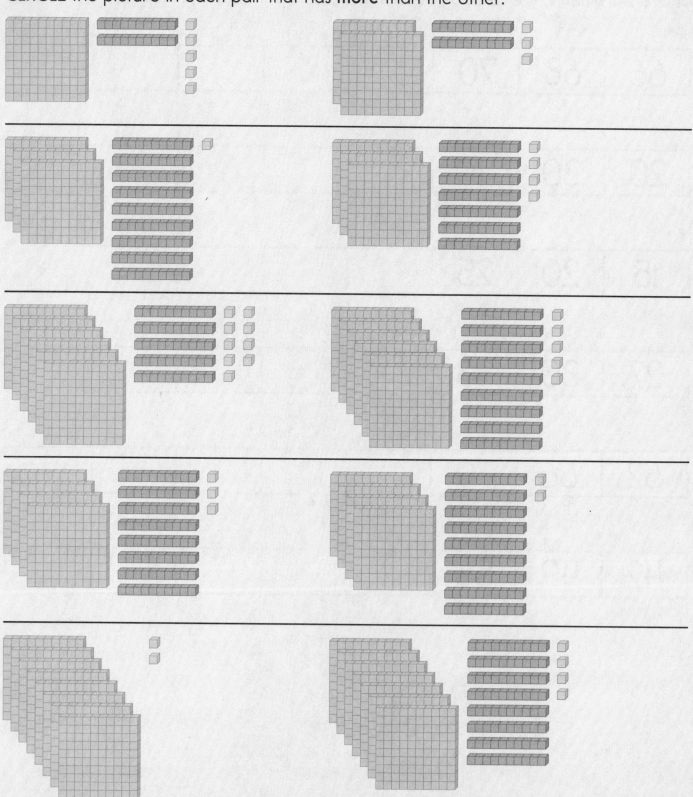

Circle It

CIRCLE the number that is **less** than the number shown in the picture.

1.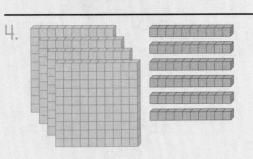

   (576)   600

2.

   329   340

3.

   713   707

4.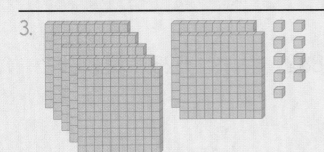

   458   464

5.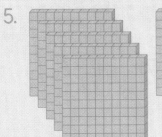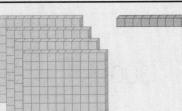

   915   910

Comparing Numbers

Mismatched

WRITE > or < in each box.

3 : 8 First, draw two dots next to the larger number.

3 · : 8 Next, draw one dot next to the smaller number.

3 < 8 Then, connect the dots.

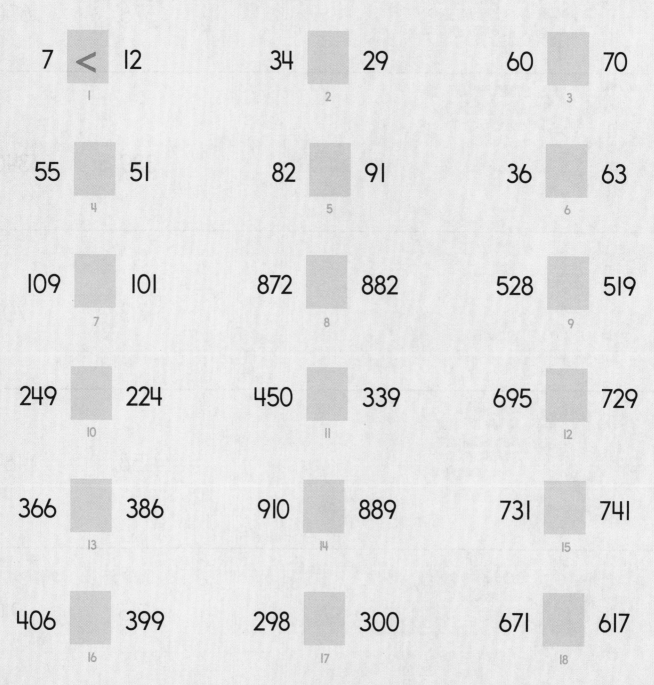

7 < 12   34 ☐ 29   60 ☐ 70
1   2   3

55 ☐ 51   82 ☐ 91   36 ☐ 63
4   5   6

109 ☐ 101 872 ☐ 882 528 ☐ 519
7   8   9

249 ☐ 224 450 ☐ 339 695 ☐ 729
10   11   12

366 ☐ 386 910 ☐ 889 731 ☐ 741
13   14   15

406 ☐ 399 298 ☐ 300 671 ☐ 617
16   17   18

Matched or Mismatched?

WRITE >, <, or = in each box.

HINT: Use = when numbers are the same.

112 >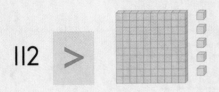
1

247
2

735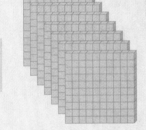
3

490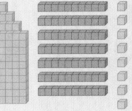
4

599
5

103
6

381
7

227
8

Round About

Rounding makes numbers easier to use.

Numbers that end in 1 through 4 get rounded **down** to the nearest ten.

Numbers that end in 5 through 9 get rounded **up** to the nearest ten.

20 21 22 23 24 25 26 27 28 29 30

20   30

ROUND each red number to the nearest ten.

10 11 12 13 14 15 16 17 18 19 20

1   2

60 61 63 64 64 65 66 67 68 69 70

3   4

30 31 32 33 34 35 36 37 38 39 40

5   6

50 51 52 53 54 55 56 57 58 59 60

7   8

Round About

Numbers that end in 1 through 49 get rounded **down** to the nearest hundred.

Numbers that end in 50 through 99 get rounded **up** to the nearest hundred.

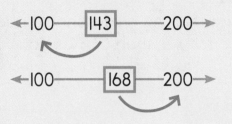

ROUND each number to the nearest hundred.

1. 689

2. 906

3. 415

4. 279

5. 538

6. 391

7. 155

8. 748

9. 332

10. 873

11. 650

12. 942

Guess and Check

Estimating is making a reasonable guess about something. GUESS the number of cubes in each set, then CHECK your guess by counting the cubes.

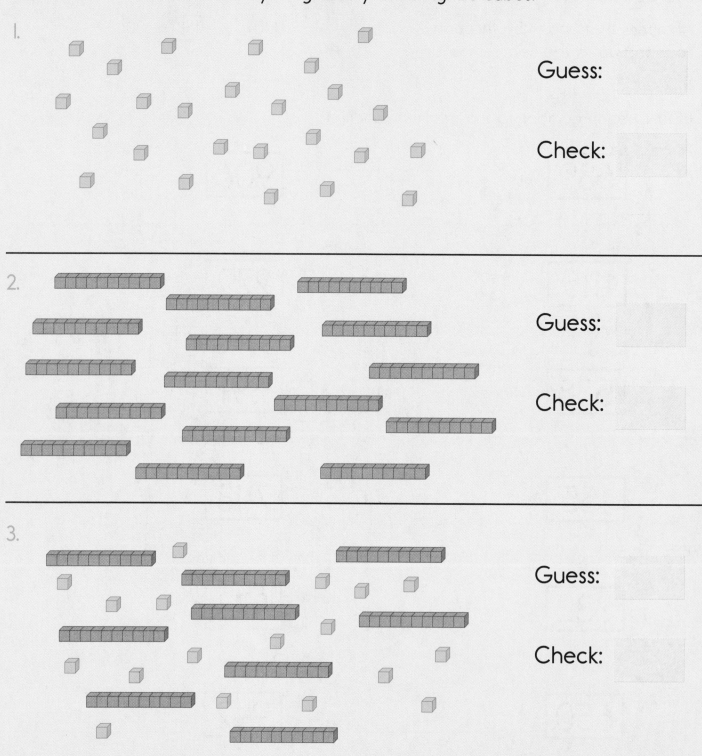

1.

Guess:

Check:

2.

Guess:

Check:

3.

Guess:

Check:

Loop It

GUESS the number of bugs. Then CIRCLE groups of five to count the bugs and check your guess.

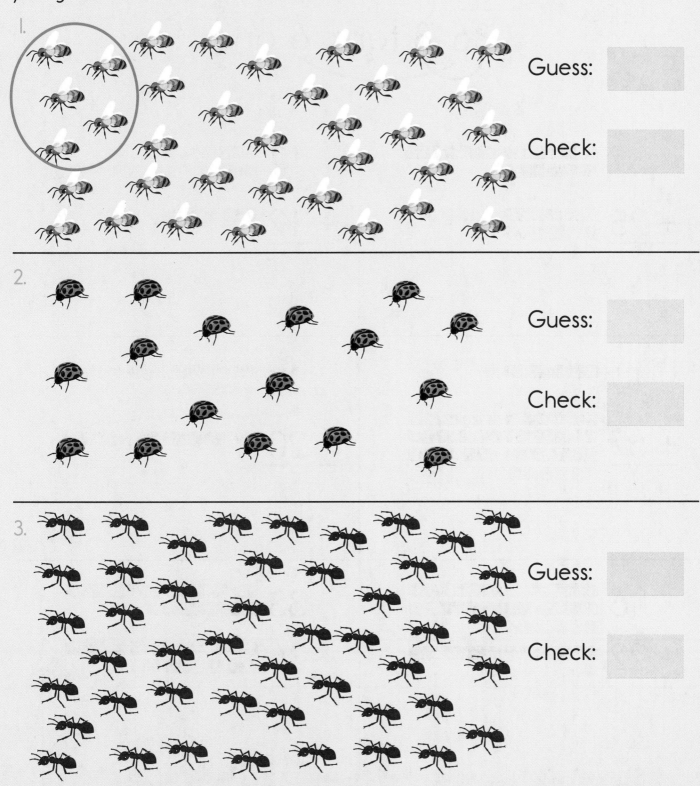

1.

Guess:

Check:

2.

Guess:

Check:

3.

Guess:

Check:

Adding

Picture It

WRITE each sum.

52

\+ 34

86 8 tens, 6 ones

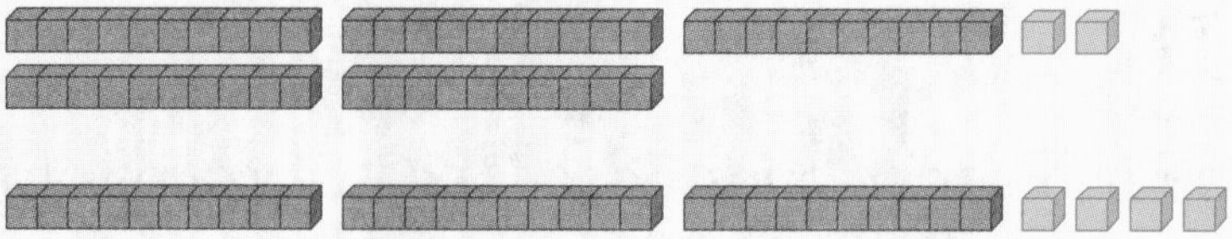

1. 31

    \+ 25

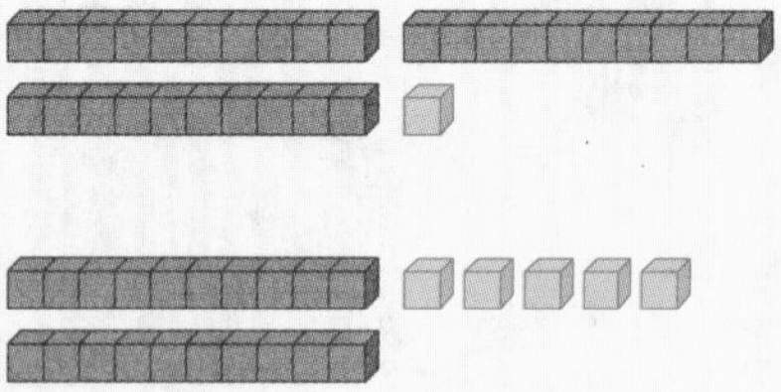

2. 17

    \+ 12

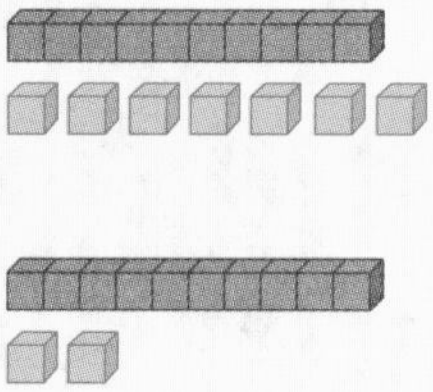

3. 11

    \+ 67

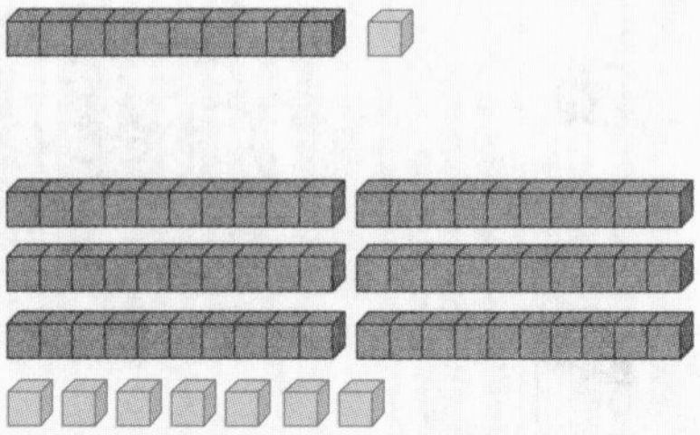

4. 24

    \+ 20

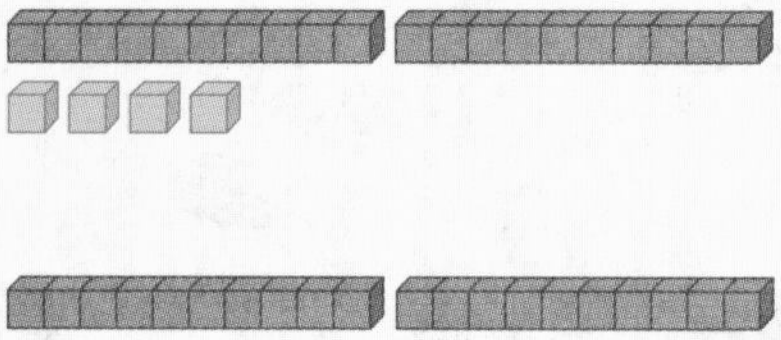

5. 46

    \+ 22

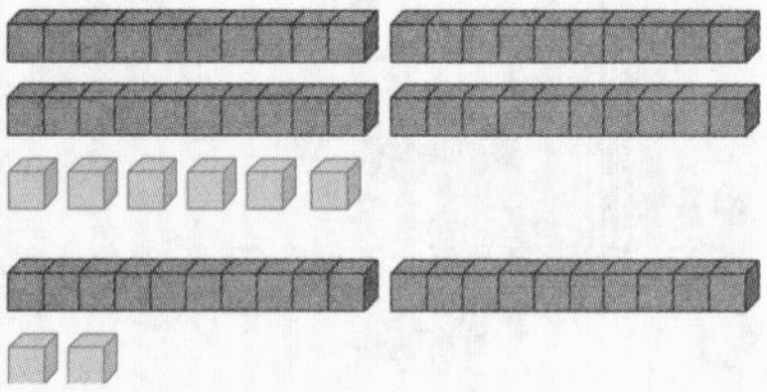

6. 33

    \+ 36

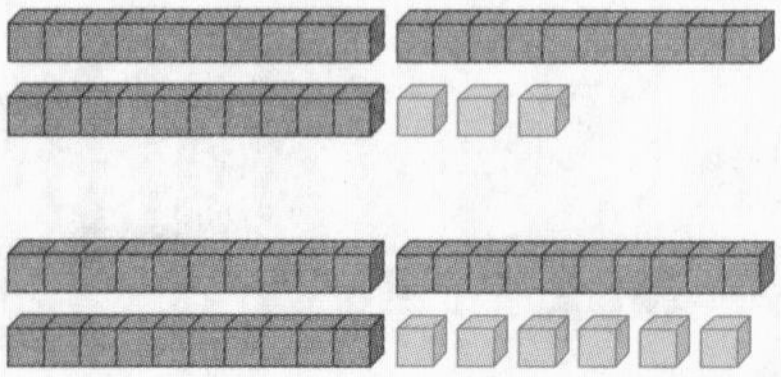

Cash Crunch

WRITE each sum.

1.

$$21¢ \quad + \quad 41¢ \quad = \quad \boxed{} ¢$$

2.

$$81¢ \quad + \quad 15¢ \quad = \quad \boxed{} ¢$$

3.

$$23¢ \quad + \quad 21¢ \quad = \quad \boxed{} ¢$$

4.

$$57¢ \quad + \quad 32¢ \quad = \quad \boxed{} ¢$$

5.

$$33¢ \quad + \quad 24¢ \quad = \quad \boxed{} ¢$$

6.

$$27¢ \quad + \quad 52¢ \quad = \quad \boxed{} ¢$$

Adding

It All Adds Up

WRITE each sum.

1. $\begin{array}{r} 62 \\ + 17 \\ \hline \end{array}$

2. $\begin{array}{r} 13 \\ + 41 \\ \hline \end{array}$

3. $\begin{array}{r} 88 \\ + 10 \\ \hline \end{array}$

4. $\begin{array}{r} 55 \\ + 32 \\ \hline \end{array}$

5. $\begin{array}{r} 22 \\ + 22 \\ \hline \end{array}$

6. $\begin{array}{r} 20 \\ + 19 \\ \hline \end{array}$

7. $\begin{array}{r} 64 \\ + 12 \\ \hline \end{array}$

8. $\begin{array}{r} 43 \\ + 26 \\ \hline \end{array}$

9. 44 + 33 =

10. 30 + 18 =

11. 10 + 21 =

12. 25 + 72 =

13. 18 + 41 =

14. 80 + 14 =

15. 32 + 32 =

16. 54 + 35 =

It All Adds Up

WRITE each missing number.

1.   65
    + ☐
    ———
    75

2.   38
    + ☐
    ———
    59

3.   14
    + ☐
    ———
    26

4.   53
    + ☐
    ———
    98

5.   41
    + ☐
    ———
    83

6.   11
    + ☐
    ———
    76

7.   25
    + ☐
    ———
    97

8.   70
    + ☐
    ———
    88

9.   ☐ + 77 = 99

10.   50 + ☐ = 63

11.   31 + ☐ = 82

12.   ☐ + 16 = 59

13.   ☐ + 40 = 72

14.   64 + ☐ = 95

15.   12 + ☐ = 34

16.   ☐ + 81 = 93

Subtracting

Picture It

WRITE each difference.

$$37$$
$$-\ 12$$

$$25 \quad \text{2 tens, 5 ones}$$

1.
$$74$$
$$-\ 31$$

2.
$$58$$
$$-\ 26$$

3.
$$95$$
$$-\ 43$$

4.
$$89$$
$$-\ 64$$

5.
$$35$$
$$-\ 22$$

6.
$$77$$
$$-\ 16$$

Cash Crunch

WRITE each difference.

HINT: Cross out dimes and pennies to help you subtract.

1.

48¢   –   13¢   =   35 ¢

2.

64¢   –   33¢   =   ¢

3.

81¢   –   21¢   =   ¢

4.

38¢   –   26¢   =   ¢

5.

99¢   –   73¢   =   ¢

6.

83¢   –   42¢   =   ¢

Subtracting

What's the Difference?

WRITE each difference.

1.   59
   − 32

2.   36
   − 26

3.   62
   − 41

4.   87
   − 75

5.   91
   − 10

6.   48
   − 23

7.   76
   − 14

8.   58
   − 45

9. $60 - 20 =$

10. $39 - 28 =$

11. $46 - 16 =$

12. $55 - 31 =$

13. $73 - 21 =$

14. $28 - 13 =$

15. $95 - 23 =$

16. $88 - 57 =$

What's the Difference?

WRITE each missing number.

1.
$$90$$
$$-\ \boxed{}$$
$$40$$

2.
$$79$$
$$-\ \boxed{}$$
$$33$$

3.
$$24$$
$$-\ \boxed{}$$
$$12$$

4.
$$56$$
$$-\ \boxed{}$$
$$41$$

5.
$$63$$
$$-\ \boxed{}$$
$$22$$

6.
$$85$$
$$-\ \boxed{}$$
$$65$$

7.
$$37$$
$$-\ \boxed{}$$
$$10$$

8.
$$92$$
$$-\ \boxed{}$$
$$71$$

9. $\boxed{} - 23 = 72$

10. $45 - \boxed{} = 11$

11. $83 - \boxed{} = 53$

12. $\boxed{} - 19 = 50$

13. $\boxed{} - 11 = 64$

14. $68 - \boxed{} = 44$

15. $78 - \boxed{} = 21$

16. $\boxed{} - 32 = 16$

Adding with Regrouping

Picture It

WRITE each sum.

$$26$$
$$+\ 45$$

6 tens, 11 ones

71   7 tens, 1 one

11 ones = 1 ten, 1 one

1. $$19$$
   $$+\ 23$$

2. $$56$$
   $$+\ 37$$

3. $$48$$
   $$+\ 34$$

4. $$36$$
   $$+\ 29$$

5. $$78$$
   $$+\ 13$$

6. $$53$$
   $$+\ 17$$

Cash Crunch

WRITE each sum.

HINT: Remember that the value of ten pennies equals one dime.

1. 16¢   +   49¢   =   ¢

2. 74¢   +   18¢   =   ¢

3. 29¢   +   41¢   =   ¢

4. 35¢   +   46¢   =   ¢

5. 25¢   +   27¢   =   ¢

6. 58¢   +   15¢   =   ¢

Adding with Regrouping

It All Adds Up

WRITE each sum.

| $\begin{array}{r} 29 \\ +13 \\ \hline \end{array}$ | First, add the numbers in the ones place. $9 + 3 = 12$ | $\begin{array}{r} ^1\ 29 \\ +13 \\ \hline 2 \end{array}$ | Write a 2 in the ones place, and write a 1 in the tens place. | $\begin{array}{r} ^1\ 29 \\ +13 \\ \hline 42 \end{array}$ | Then add the tens. $1 + 2 + 1 = 4$. Write 4 in the tens place. $29 + 13 = 42$ |

1. $\begin{array}{r} 26 \\ +35 \\ \hline \end{array}$

2. $\begin{array}{r} 62 \\ +19 \\ \hline \end{array}$

3. $\begin{array}{r} 75 \\ +15 \\ \hline \end{array}$

4. $\begin{array}{r} 37 \\ +54 \\ \hline \end{array}$

5. $\begin{array}{r} 48 \\ +22 \\ \hline \end{array}$

6. $\begin{array}{r} 37 \\ +37 \\ \hline \end{array}$

7. $\begin{array}{r} 17 \\ +18 \\ \hline \end{array}$

8. $\begin{array}{r} 39 \\ +19 \\ \hline \end{array}$

9. $\begin{array}{r} 16 \\ +16 \\ \hline \end{array}$

10. $\begin{array}{r} 66 \\ +14 \\ \hline \end{array}$

11. $\begin{array}{r} 28 \\ +38 \\ \hline \end{array}$

12. $\begin{array}{r} 58 \\ +34 \\ \hline \end{array}$

It All Adds Up

WRITE each sum.

1. 47 + 13 =

2. 18 + 57 =

3. 24 + 68 =

4. 48 + 19 =

5. 36 + 54 =

6. 27 + 14 =

7. 49 + 33 =

8. 11 + 39 =

9. 54 + 17 =

10. 35 + 29 =

11. 79 + 21 =

12. 48 + 47 =

Subtracting with Regrouping

Picture It

WRITE each difference.

$$42$$
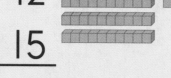

$$-15$$

$$27 \quad \text{2 tens, 7 ones}$$

1. 93
   -26
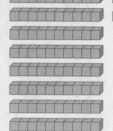

2. 70
   -54

3. 76
   -37

4. 81
   -8

5. 66
   -48
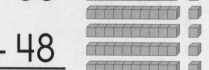

6. 52
   -25
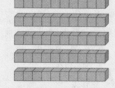

8

Picture It

WRITE each difference.

HINT: Color the number of cubes being subtracted, then count the number of cubes remaining.

1.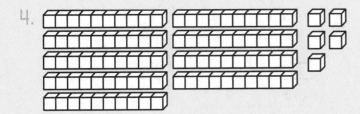

$$84 - 56 =$$

2.

$$36 - 18 =$$

3.

$$61 - 22 =$$

4.

$$95 - 29 =$$

5.

$$73 - 58 =$$

6.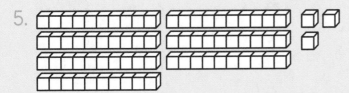

$$62 - 5 =$$

Subtracting with Regrouping

What's the Difference?

WRITE each difference.

53 −16	First, regroup from the tens place. Cross out the 5 and write 4, and cross out the 3 and write 13.	⁴ ¹³ 5̶3̶ −16 7	Subtract in the ones place: 13 − 6 = 7. Write 7 in the ones place.	⁴ ¹³ 5̶3̶ −16 37	Then, subtract in the tens place: 4 − 1 = 3. Write 3 in the tens place. 53 − 16 = 37

1. $\begin{array}{r} 78 \\ -19 \\ \hline \end{array}$

2. $\begin{array}{r} 35 \\ -27 \\ \hline \end{array}$

3. $\begin{array}{r} 44 \\ -15 \\ \hline \end{array}$

4. $\begin{array}{r} 30 \\ -12 \\ \hline \end{array}$

5. $\begin{array}{r} 85 \\ -47 \\ \hline \end{array}$

6. $\begin{array}{r} 93 \\ -68 \\ \hline \end{array}$

7. $\begin{array}{r} 82 \\ -56 \\ \hline \end{array}$

8. $\begin{array}{r} 73 \\ -18 \\ \hline \end{array}$

9. $\begin{array}{r} 63 \\ -26 \\ \hline \end{array}$

10. $\begin{array}{r} 95 \\ -86 \\ \hline \end{array}$

11. $\begin{array}{r} 64 \\ -36 \\ \hline \end{array}$

12. $\begin{array}{r} 47 \\ -28 \\ \hline \end{array}$

What's the Difference?

WRITE each difference.

1. $52 - 35 =$

2. $61 - 57 =$

3. $98 - 19 =$

4. $74 - 17 =$

5. $47 - 28 =$

6. $51 - 13 =$

7. $41 - 18 =$

8. $80 - 39 =$

9. $65 - 26 =$

10. $72 - 25 =$

11. $90 - 16 =$

12. $54 - 45 =$

Grouping

Pick a Package

How many bags of five marbles can be made from the loose marbles? WRITE the answer.

HINT: Draw circles around groups of five, and count the number of groups you have.

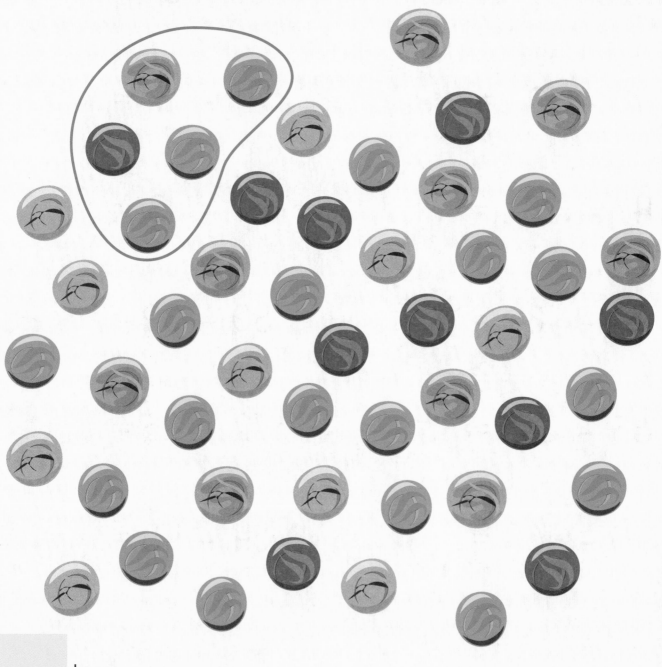

bags

9

Pick a Package

Each seed packet comes with eight seeds. How many packets are needed to hold the seeds? How many seeds are there? WRITE the answers.

HINT: Draw circles around groups of eight, and use the groups to help you count the seeds.

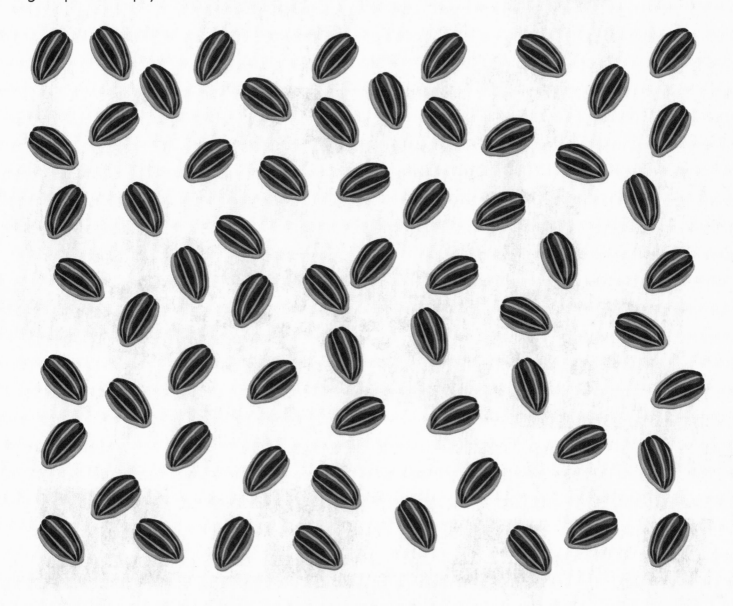

seed packets for   seeds

Pick a Package

How many of each type of box would be needed to pack the chocolates on the conveyor belt? WRITE the answer below each box.

1

2

3

4

Games Galore

WRITE the total number of game parts you see in the four games.

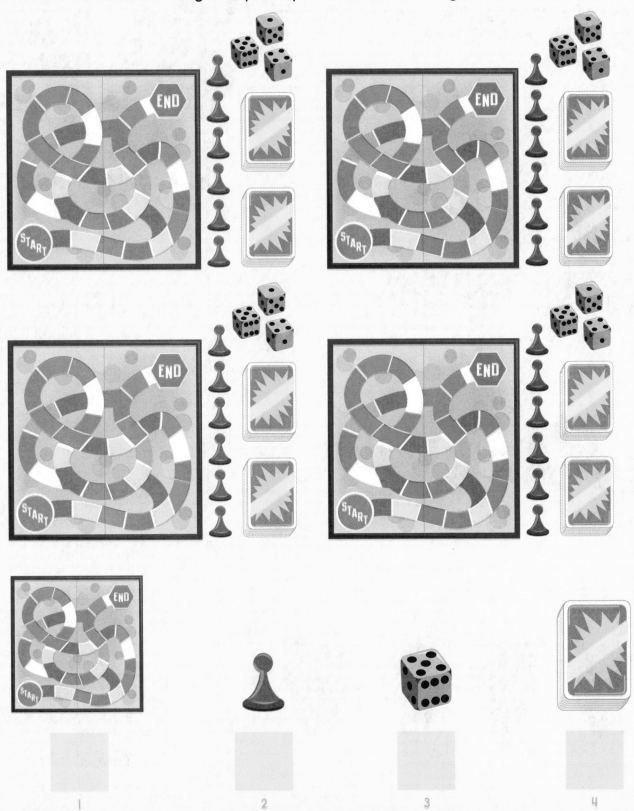

1	2	3	4

Fair Share

The twins aren't happy unless they get the same number of everything. How many of each treat will they each get? WRITE the answer.

cupcakes

cookies

milk shakes

Fair Share

If the same number of cards is dealt to every player, how many cards will each player get? WRITE the answer.

cards

Fair Share

WRITE the number of gems each pirate will get if they split the treasure equally.

1

2

3

4

Fair Share

A family of five is having dinner, and everyone can eat the same amount of food. If each type of food is shared equally, how many pieces of each will a person get? How many pieces will be left over?
WRITE the answers.

1.

| | piece of chicken | | left over |

2.

| | French fries | | left over |

3.

| | green beans | | left over |

Odd or Even?

An even number of items can be shared equally by two people. An odd number of items cannot be shared equally by two people. There will always be one extra item. CIRCLE **odd** or **even** for each group.

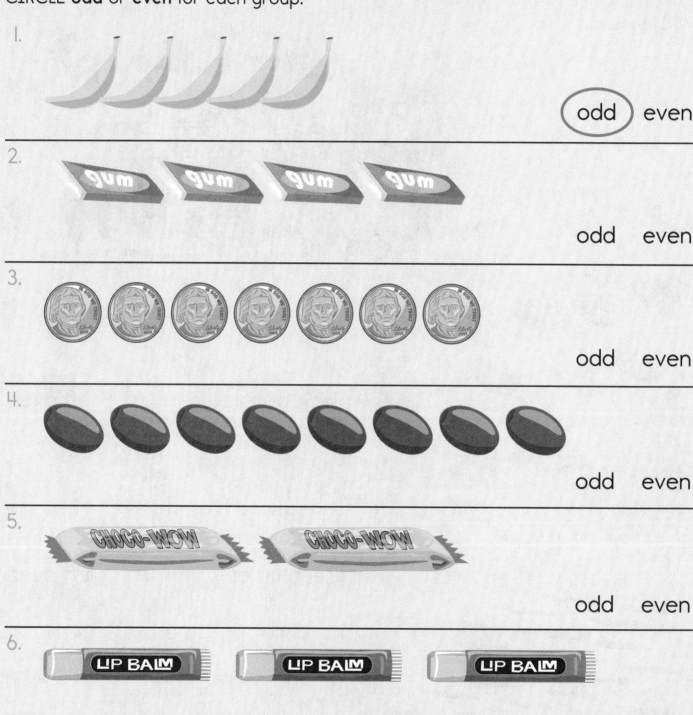

1.

(odd) even

2.

odd   even

3.

odd   even

4.

odd   even

5.

odd   even

6.

odd   even

Card Tricks

CIRCLE all of the cards with even numbers.

  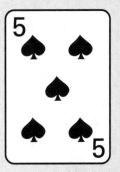

Recognizing Fractions

Piece of Cake

COLOR the cake pieces to match each fraction.

Example: $\frac{1}{4}$ ← colored piece
← pieces total

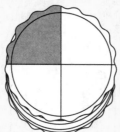

$\frac{1}{2}$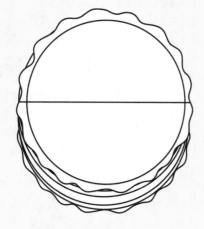

$\frac{1}{3}$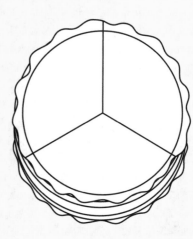

$\frac{2}{4}$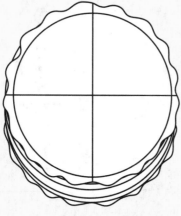

$\frac{2}{2}$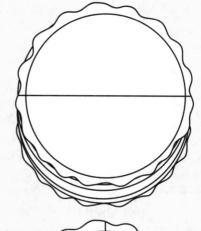

$\frac{2}{3}$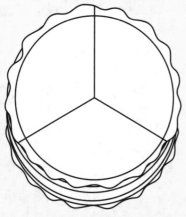

$\frac{3}{4}$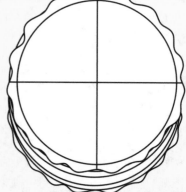

Fraction Bars

WRITE the fraction for each picture.

Example:

$\dfrac{2}{3}$ ← colored sections
← total sections

1. _____

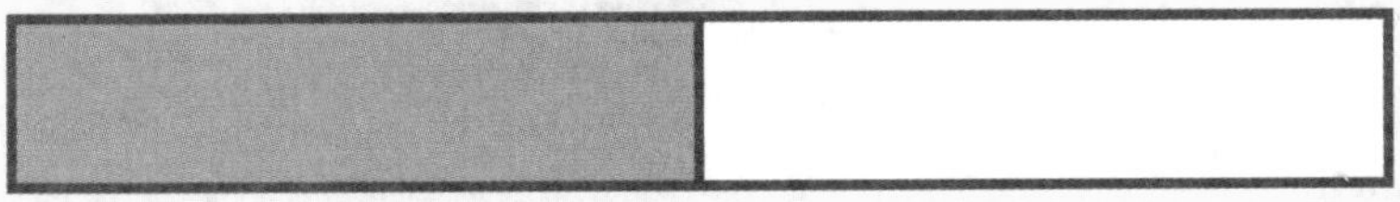

2. _____

3. _____

4. _____

5. _____

6. _____

Recognizing Fractions

Match Up

DRAW lines to connect the fractions and pictures that go together.

$\dfrac{2}{3}$

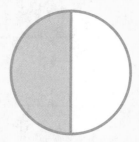

$\dfrac{1}{4}$

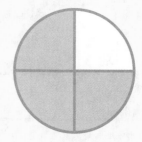

$\dfrac{1}{2}$

$\dfrac{3}{4}$

$\dfrac{1}{3}$

Color the Shapes

COLOR the part or parts of each shape to match the fraction.

$\dfrac{3}{4}$

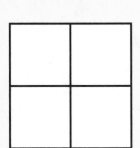

$\dfrac{2}{3}$

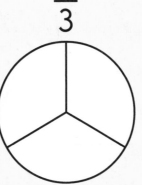

$\dfrac{1}{3}$

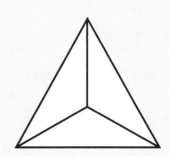

$\dfrac{1}{4}$

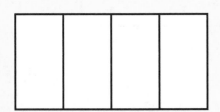

$\dfrac{1}{2}$

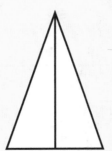

$\dfrac{4}{4}$

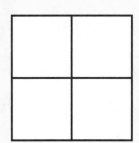

Piece of Cake

COLOR the cake pieces to match each fraction. Then CIRCLE the larger fraction.

HINT: The larger fraction is the one with more of the cake colored.

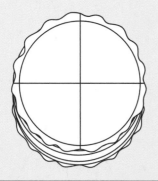 $\dfrac{1}{4}$

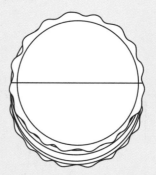 $\dfrac{1}{2}$

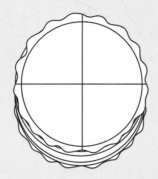 $\dfrac{2}{4}$

 $\dfrac{2}{3}$

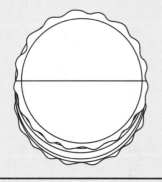 $\dfrac{1}{2}$

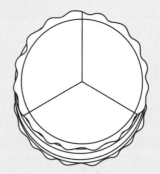 $\dfrac{1}{3}$

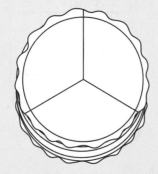 $\dfrac{2}{3}$

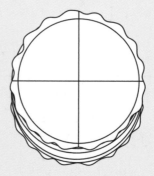 $\dfrac{3}{4}$

Fraction Bars

WRITE the fraction for each picture. Then CIRCLE the smaller fraction.

1.

____   ____

2.

____   ____

3.

____   ____

4.

____   ____

Pizza Party

DRAW a line to match each person to the correct slice of pizza.
Then WRITE answers to the questions.

Alex

I want $\frac{1}{3}$ of a pizza.

Ellie

I want $\frac{3}{4}$ of a pizza.

Kiki

I want $\frac{1}{2}$ of a pizza.

Miles

I want $\frac{1}{4}$ of a pizza.

1. Who has the largest slice of pizza? _____

2. Who has the smallest slice of pizza? _____

Matched or Mismatched?

WRITE >, <, or = in each box.

HINT: Use these fraction circles to help you picture the fractions.

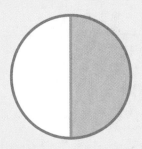 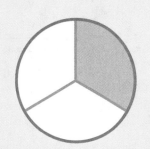 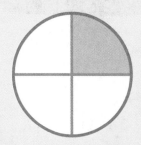

$\dfrac{1}{4}$ ☐ $\dfrac{1}{3}$ 1 $\dfrac{2}{2}$ ☐ $\dfrac{2}{3}$ 2 $\dfrac{2}{4}$ ☐ $\dfrac{1}{2}$ 3

$\dfrac{3}{4}$ ☐ $\dfrac{1}{2}$ 4 $\dfrac{1}{2}$ ☐ $\dfrac{1}{3}$ 5 $\dfrac{3}{3}$ ☐ $\dfrac{3}{4}$ 6

$\dfrac{1}{4}$ ☐ $\dfrac{1}{2}$ 7 $\dfrac{4}{4}$ ☐ $\dfrac{3}{3}$ 8 $\dfrac{1}{2}$ ☐ $\dfrac{2}{3}$ 9

$\dfrac{2}{3}$ ☐ $\dfrac{2}{4}$ 10 $\dfrac{3}{4}$ ☐ $\dfrac{1}{3}$ 11 $\dfrac{2}{3}$ ☐ $\dfrac{3}{4}$ 12

Nonstandard Units

Measure Up

MEASURE the length of each object in paper clips.

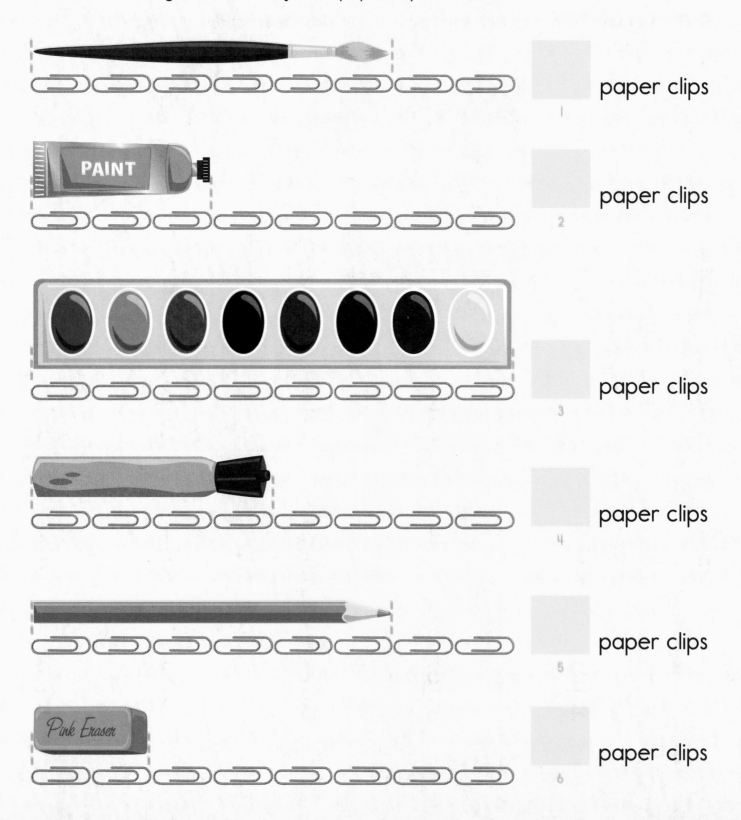

paper clips

paper clips

paper clips

paper clips

paper clips

paper clips

Measure Up

MEASURE the length of each object in dimes.

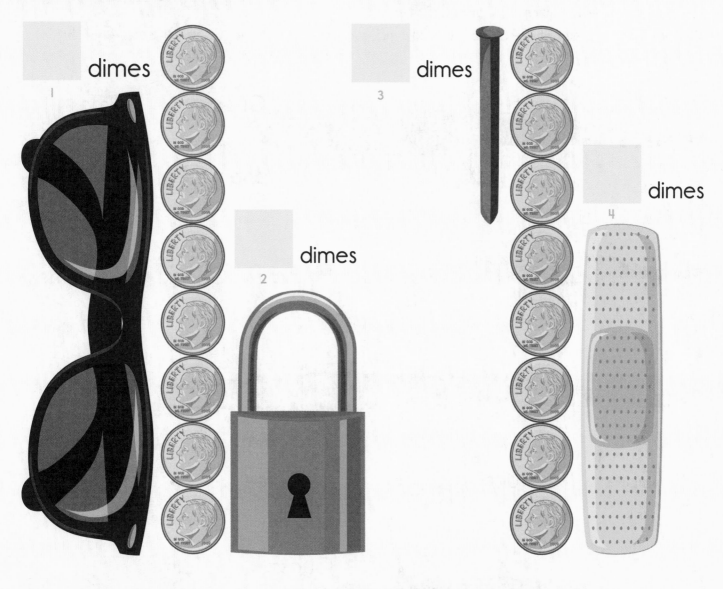

dimes
1

dimes
2

dimes
3

dimes
4

dimes
5

Nonstandard Units

Dime Line

The lizard at the top is 5 dimes long. GUESS the length of each lizard in dimes. Then LINE UP some dimes, and MEASURE each lizard.

1.

Guess: ☐ dimes

Check: ☐ dimes

2.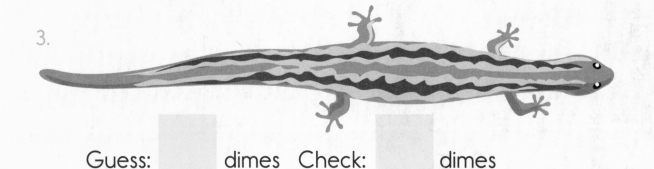

Guess: ☐ dimes   Check: ☐ dimes

3.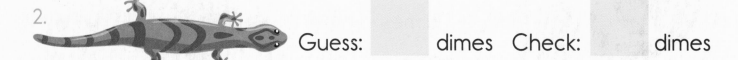

Guess: ☐ dimes   Check: ☐ dimes

4.

Guess: ☐ dimes

Check: ☐ dimes

5.

Guess: ☐ dimes

Check: ☐ dimes

Dime Line

Each piece of yarn needs to be cut to a particular length. First, DRAW a line on each piece, estimating where it will be cut. Then MEASURE using dimes, and DRAW a line in the correct place. How good was your estimate?

5 dimes

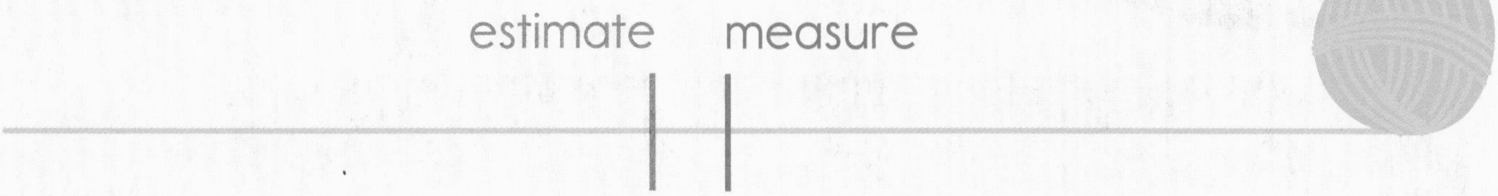

estimate   measure

8 dimes

2 dimes

6 dimes

9 dimes

3 dimes

Measure Up

MEASURE the length of each object in inches.

HINT: *Inch* and *inches* are abbreviated as *in.*

1.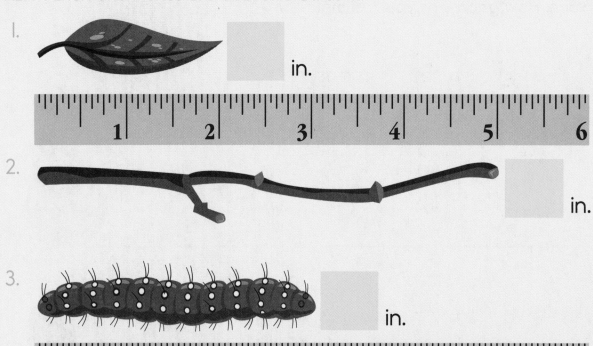

        in.

2.

        in.

3.   in.

4.   in.

5.   in.

6.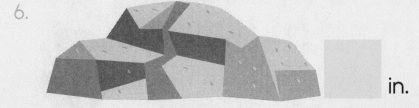

        in.

Measure Up

MEASURE the approximate height of each flower in inches.

HINT: To find the approximate height, measure each flower and find the closest number on the ruler.

about [ ] in.

1

about [ ] in.

2

about [ ] in.

3

about [ ] in.

4

Rulers Rule

The candy at the top is 4 inches long. GUESS the length of each piece of candy in inches. Then MEASURE each one with a ruler to check your guess.

1.

Guess: in.   Check: in.

2.

Guess: in.   Check: in.

3.

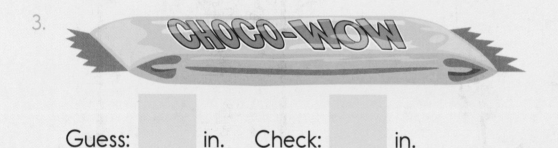

Guess: in.   Check: in.

4.

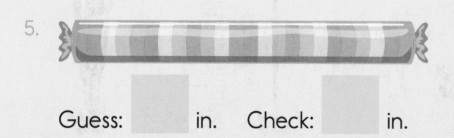

Guess: in.   Check: in.

5.

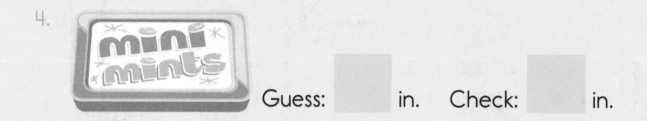

Guess: in.   Check: in.

Rulers Rule

Each piece of yarn needs to be cut to a particular length. First, DRAW a line on each piece, estimating where it will be cut. Then MEASURE with a ruler, and DRAW a line in the correct place. How good was your estimate?

3 in.

1 in.

6 in.

4 in.

2 in.

5 in.

Centimeters

Measure Up

MEASURE the length of each ribbon in centimeters.

HINT: *Centimeter(s)* is abbreviated as *cm*.

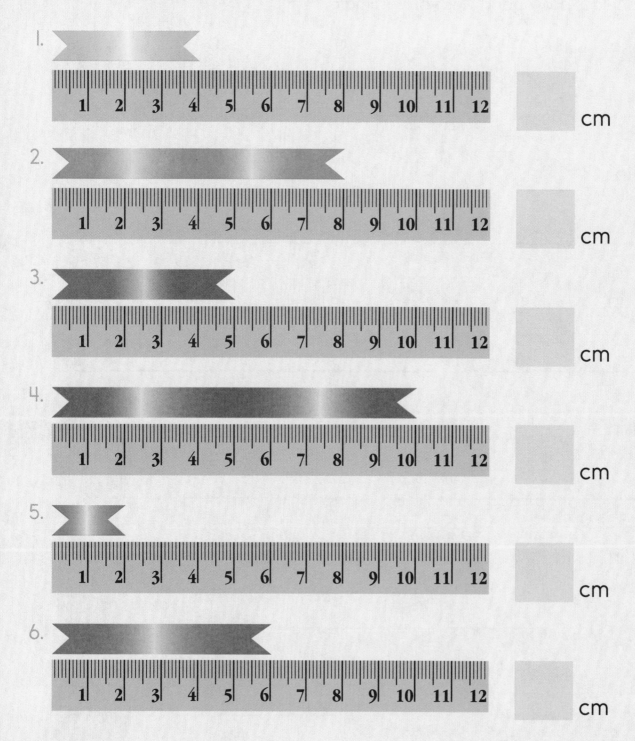

1. _____ cm

2. _____ cm

3. _____ cm

4. _____ cm

5. _____ cm

6. _____ cm

Measure Up

MEASURE the approximate height of each action figure in centimeters.

Centimeters

Rulers Rule

The worm at the top is 10 centimeters long. GUESS the length of each worm in centimeters. Then MEASURE each worm with a ruler to check your guess.

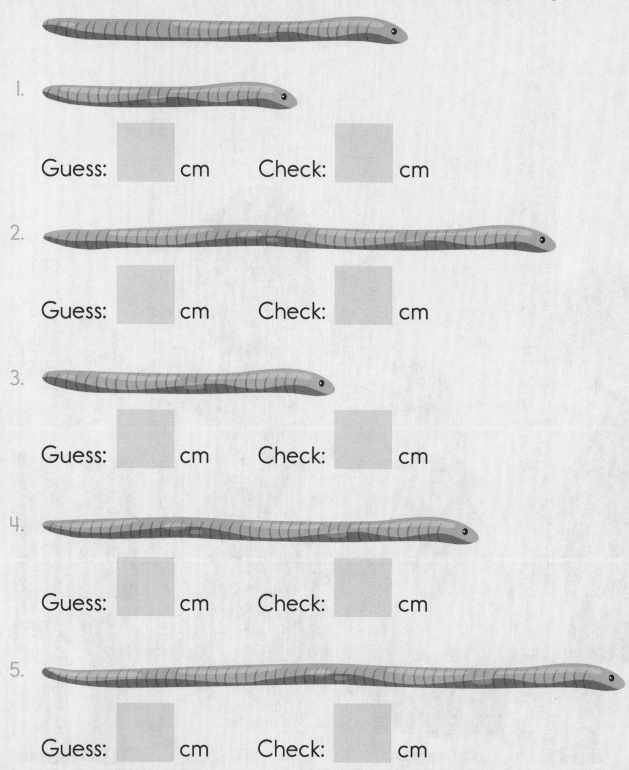

1. Guess: ___ cm   Check: ___ cm

2. Guess: ___ cm   Check: ___ cm

3. Guess: ___ cm   Check: ___ cm

4. Guess: ___ cm   Check: ___ cm

5. Guess: ___ cm   Check: ___ cm

Rulers Rule

Each piece of yarn needs to be cut to a particular length. First, DRAW a line on each piece, estimating where it will be cut. Then MEASURE with a ruler, and DRAW a line in the correct place. How good was your estimate?

6 cm

4 cm

2 cm

9 cm

7 cm

3 cm

Around We Go

Perimeter is the distance around a two-dimensional shape. WRITE the perimeter of each shape.

Example:

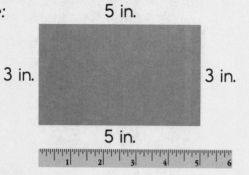

To find the perimeter, add the length of all of the sides.

5 + 3 + 5 + 3 = 16

The perimeter of this rectangle is 16 inches.

1.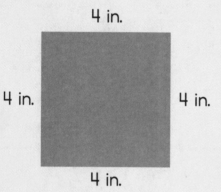

___ in.

2.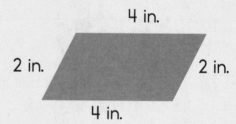

___ in.

3.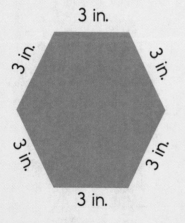

___ in.

4.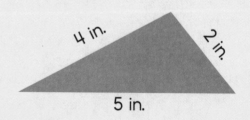

___ in.

Around We Go

MEASURE the length of each side of the shape in centimeters. Then WRITE the perimeter of the shape.

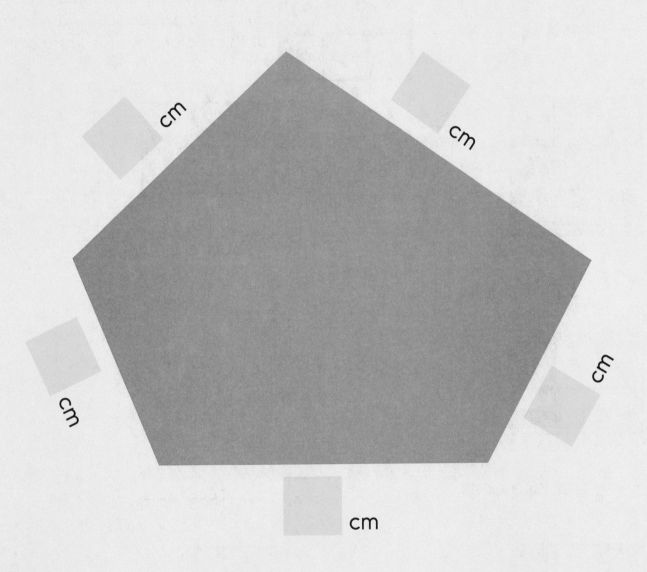

cm

cm

cm

cm

cm

Perimeter: _____ cm

Squared Away

Area is the size of the surface of a shape, and it is measured in square units.
WRITE the area of each shape.

Example: 1 square unit

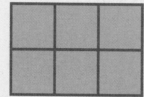 To measure the area, count the number of square units. The area of this rectangle is 6 square units.

1.

_____ square units

2.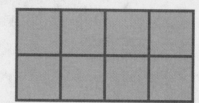

_____ square units

3.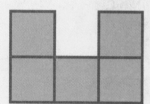

_____ square units

4.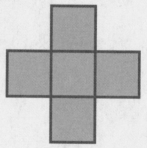

_____ square units

5.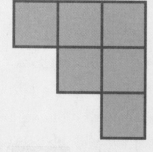

_____ square units

6.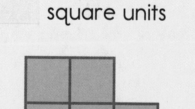

_____ square units

Which One?

CIRCLE the shape that matches each area measurement.

1.

4 square units

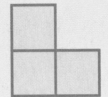 

2.

7 square units

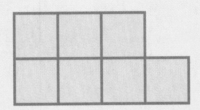 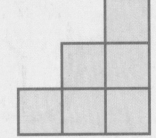

3.

5 square units

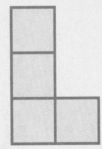 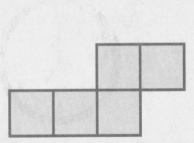

4.

6 square units

 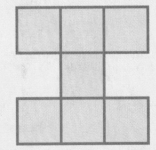

What Time Is It?

WRITE the time on each clock.

Examples:

4 : 00

8 : 30

1.

:

2.

:

3.

:

4.

:

5.

:

6.

:

Watch It!

DRAW a line to connect each watch to a clock that shows the same time.

Hours & Half Hours

Give Me a Hand

DRAW the clock hands to match the time.

1.

1:30

2.

4:00

3.

6:00

4.

8:30

5.

5:30

6.

3:00

7.

11:30

8.
7:30

Passing the Time

DRAW the time on the last clock to complete the pattern.

1.

2.

3.

4.

What Time Is It?

WRITE the time on each clock.

Examples:

 1 : 15

 5 : 45

1.  ___ : ___

2.  ___ : ___

3.  ___ : ___

4.  ___ : ___

5.  ___ : ___

6.  ___ : ___

Watch It!

DRAW a line to connect each watch to a clock that shows the same time.

Give Me a Hand

DRAW the clock hands to match the time.

1.

4:15

2.

12:45

3.

7:15

4.

1:45

5.

10:45

6.

5:15

7.

8:15

8.

2:45

Passing the Time

DRAW the time on the last clock to complete the pattern.

1.

2.

3.

4.

15-Minute Warning

Mom says you're leaving in 15 minutes.
WRITE the time you need to go.

1.  + 15 minutes = : ☐

2.  + 15 minutes = : ☐

3.  + 15 minutes = : ☐

4.  + 15 minutes = : ☐

Set Your Clock

Each clock is slow. DRAW hands to show the correct time on each clock.

HINT: Add time to each clock.

1.  2 hours slow ➝

2.  30 minutes slow ➝

3.  15 minutes slow ➝

4.  45 minutes slow ➝

Set Your Clock

Each clock is fast. DRAW hands to show the correct time on each clock.

HINT: Subtract time from each clock.

1.  15 minutes fast ⟶

2.  3 hours fast ⟶

3.  45 minutes fast ⟶

4.  30 minutes fast ⟶

Time Difference

WRITE the difference in time between each pair of clocks.

1.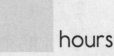

   hours   minutes

2.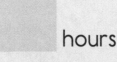

   hours   minutes

3.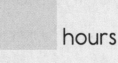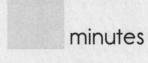

   hours   minutes

4.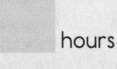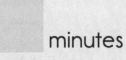

   hours   minutes

Calendars

Save the Date

CIRCLE the correct answer.

Month

NOVEMBER						
S	M	T	W	T	F	S
	1	2	3	4	5	6
7	8	9	10	11	12	13
14	15	16	17	18	19	20
21	22	22	23	25	26	27
28	29	30				

Days of the week:
Sunday
Monday
Tuesday
Wednesday
Thursday
Friday
Saturday

1. What month is this?

December   July   November

2. How many days are in this month?

29   30   31

3. What is the first day of this month?

Monday   Thursday   Saturday

4. What is the date of the first Friday?

November 1   November 5   November 12

5. How many Mondays are in this month?

3   4   5

6. How many Fridays are in this month?

3   4   5

Save the Date

WRITE the correct answer.

JANUARY	FEBRUARY	MARCH	APRIL	MAY	JUNE
S M T W T F S	S M T W T F S	S M T W T F S	S M T W T F S	S M T W T F S	S M T W T F S
1 2 3	1 2 3 4 5 6 7	1 2 3 4 5 6 7	1 2 3 4	1 2	1 2 3 4 5 6
4 5 6 7 8 9 10	8 9 10 11 12 13 14	8 9 10 11 12 13 14	5 6 7 8 9 10 11	3 4 5 6 7 8 9	7 8 9 10 11 12 13
11 12 13 14 15 16 17	15 16 17 18 19 20 21	15 16 17 18 19 20 21	12 13 14 15 16 17 18	10 11 12 13 14 15 16	14 15 16 17 18 19 20
18 19 20 21 22 23 24	22 23 24 25 26 27 28	22 23 24 25 26 27 28	19 20 21 22 23 24 25	17 18 19 20 21 22 23	21 22 23 24 25 26 27
25 26 27 28 29 30 31		29 30 31	26 27 28 29 30	24 25 26 27 28 29 30	28 29 30
				31	

JULY	AUGUST	SEPTEMBER	OCTOBER	NOVEMBER	DECEMBER
S M T W T F S	S M T W T F S	S M T W T F S	S M T W T F S	S M T W T F S	S M T W T F S
1 2 3 4	1	1 2 3 4 5	1 2 3	1 2 3 4 5 6 7	1 2 3 4 5
5 6 7 8 9 10 11	2 3 4 5 6 7 8	6 7 8 9 10 11 12	4 5 6 7 8 9 10	8 9 10 11 12 13 14	6 7 8 9 10 11 12
12 13 14 15 16 17 18	9 10 11 12 13 14 15	13 14 15 16 17 18 19	11 12 13 14 15 16 17	15 16 17 18 19 20 21	13 14 15 16 17 18 19
19 20 21 22 23 24 25	16 17 18 19 20 21 22	20 21 22 23 24 25 26	18 19 20 21 22 23 24	22 23 24 25 26 27 28	20 21 22 23 24 25 26
26 27 28 29 30 31	23 24 25 26 27 28 29	27 28 29 30	25 26 27 28 29 30 31	29 30	27 28 29 30 31
	30 31				

1. How many months are in one year? _____

2. What is the first month of the year? _____

3. Which month has 28 days? _____

4. How many months have 31 days? _____

5. What day of the week is Valentine's Day, February 14?

_____

6. On what day of the week does October begin?

_____

Save the Date

DRAW the pictures for the special events on the correct place on the calendar.

HINT: Some events last longer than one day.

Maya's beach party	July 17	(sun)
Florida vacation	July 30 to August 6	V
First day of school	August 31	1
Tyler's birthday	August 12	(balloon)
Mom and Dad's anniversary	July 29	(ring)
Dad and Tyler's fishing trip	August 21–22	(fish)
Hota Dakota concert	July 3	(music notes)
Dentist appointment	August 9	(tooth)

JULY

Sunday	Monday	Tuesday	Wednesday	Thursday	Friday	Saturday
				1	2	3
4	5	6	7	8	9	10
11	12	13	14	15	16	17
18	19	20	21	22	23	24
25	26	27	28	29	30	31

AUGUST

Sunday	Monday	Tuesday	Wednesday	Thursday	Friday	Saturday
1	2	3	4	5	6	7
8	9	10	11	12	13	14
15	16	17	18	19	20	21
22	23	24	25	26	27	28
29	30	31				

Which One?

CIRCLE the money that matches the dollar amount.

$1.42

$0.80

$1.23

$1.86

$2.06

$5.55

Match Up

DRAW lines to connect money with the same value.

Money Bags

WRITE the value of the money on the bag.

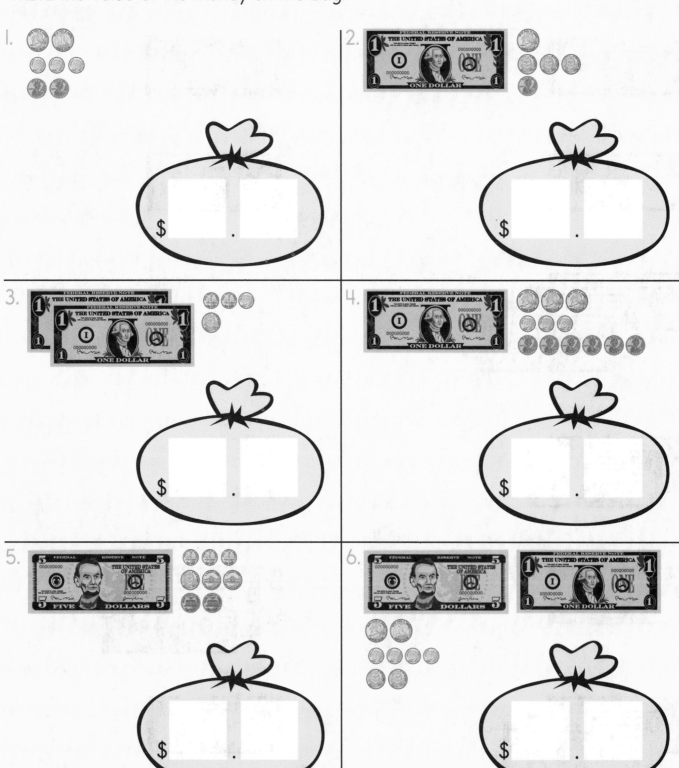

1.

2.

3.

4.

5.

6.

Odd One Out

CROSS OUT the picture or number that does **not** match the others.

$0.70

$1.16

$3.62

$5.85

Pay Up

CIRCLE the money needed to buy each item using exact change.

 **Totally Taters** $1.15

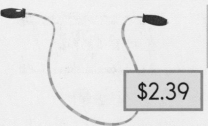 $2.39

 $3.90

 **The FUNNIEST JOKES EVER** $5.53

 $8.41

Match Up

DRAW lines to connect the money with the food that can be bought using exact change.

$2.74

$3.03

$1.99

$6.57

$2.66

Who Can Buy It?

CIRCLE the hands of the people who have enough money to buy a movie ticket.

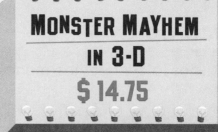

MONSTER MAYHEM IN 3-D

$ 14.75

TICKETS

Pay Up

WRITE the cost to buy all three things.

$3.20

$9.68

$15.09

Total cost $ _____ . __

Comparing Amounts

Circle It

CIRCLE all of the objects that cost **less** than the top object.

$8.93

$9.37

$10.50

$2.44

$5.89

$4.16

Matched or Mismatched?

WRITE >, <, or = in each box.

1.

2.

3.

4. $2.99

5. $4.02

6. $6.52

7. $8.85

Which Is Less?

CIRCLE the picture with **less** money than the other.

Mismatched

WRITE > or < in each box.

1.
$0.13 ☐ $0.56

2.
$5.44 ☐ $4.30

3.
$2.69 ☐ $2.07

4.
$5.21 ☐ $5.18

5.
$8.25 ☐ $9.77

6.
$3.32 ☐ $3.20

2nd Grade
Math
Games & Puzzles

Hidden Design

COUNT the hundreds, tens, and ones. Then COLOR the squares that match the numbers to see the hidden design.

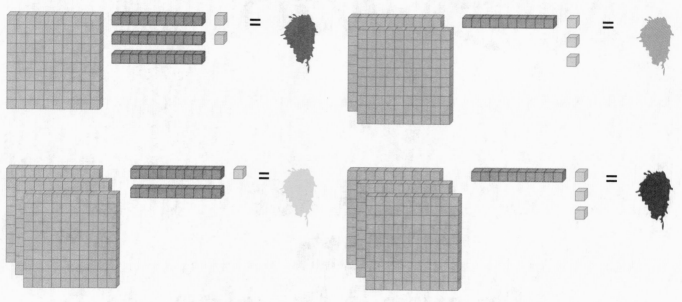

313	213	132	321	132	213	313	321
213	132	321	313	321	132	213	313
132	321	313	213	313	321	132	213
321	313	213	132	213	313	321	132
313	213	132	321	132	213	313	321
213	132	321	313	321	132	213	313
132	321	313	213	313	321	132	213
321	313	213	132	213	313	321	132

Safe Crackers

WRITE the number for each picture. Then WRITE the digit from the hundreds place of each number from left to right to find the combination for the safe.

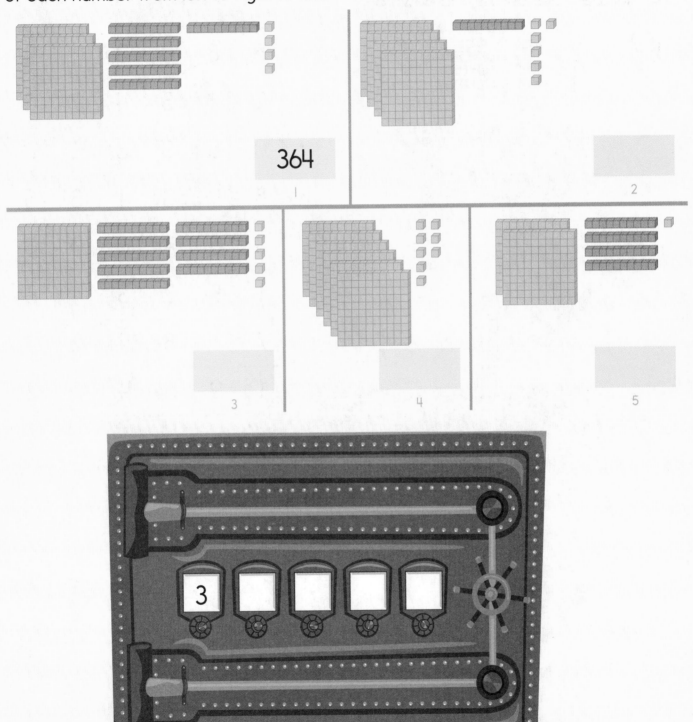

364

1

2

3

4

5

3

Place Value

Number Search

WRITE the number for each picture. Then CIRCLE it in the puzzle.

HINT: Numbers are across and down only.

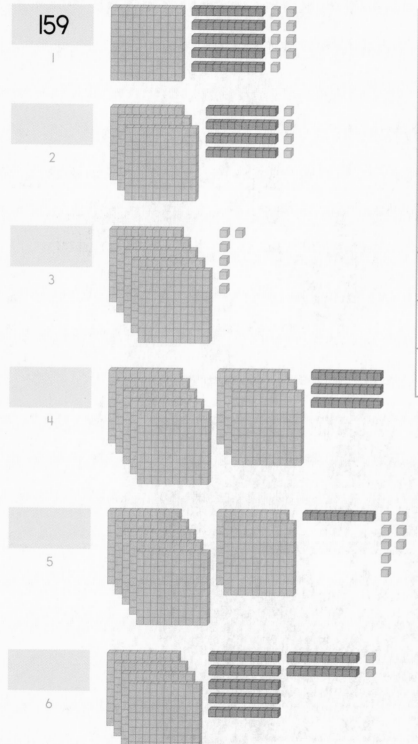

159

1

2

3

4

5

6

5	8	0	3	1	4
2	1	5	4	7	0
0	5	0	6	8	3
8	9	3	1	3	5
3	3	7	6	0	0
1	5	2	3	4	8
7	1	8	4	2	1
1	9	6	4	7	2

Roll It

ROLL a number cube, and WRITE the number in the first box. ROLL the number cube two more times, and WRITE the numbers in the second and third boxes. Then COLOR the hundreds, tens, and ones to match the number.

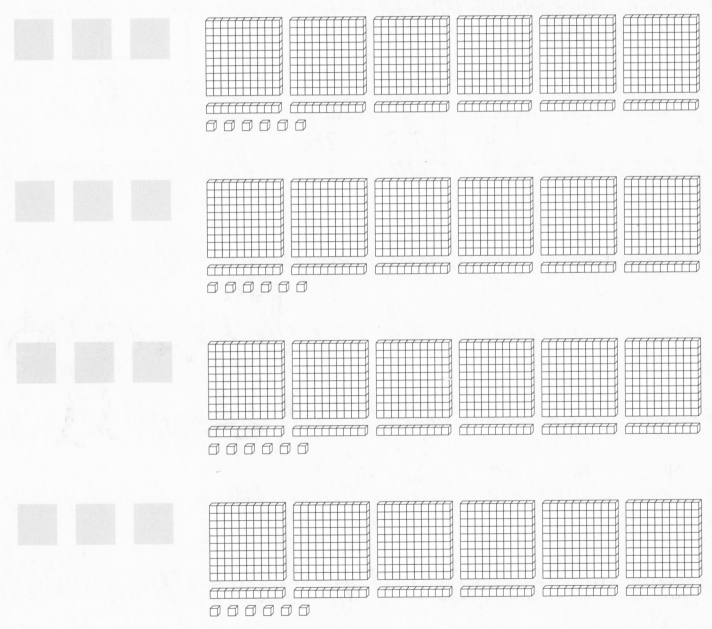

Code Breaker

WRITE the missing numbers. Then WRITE the letter that matches each number to solve the riddle.

1.

97	98	99		101	102		104
B			Y			K	

2.

213	214		216	217		219	
		I			R		U

3.

		748	749	750	751		
T	O					L	E

What did the zero say to the eight?

___ ___ ___ ___ ___
215 752 215 103 753

___ ___ ___ ___ B ___ ___ ___ ___ !
100 747 220 218   97 753 752 746

Skipping Stones

DRAW a path by skip counting by 5 to cross the river.

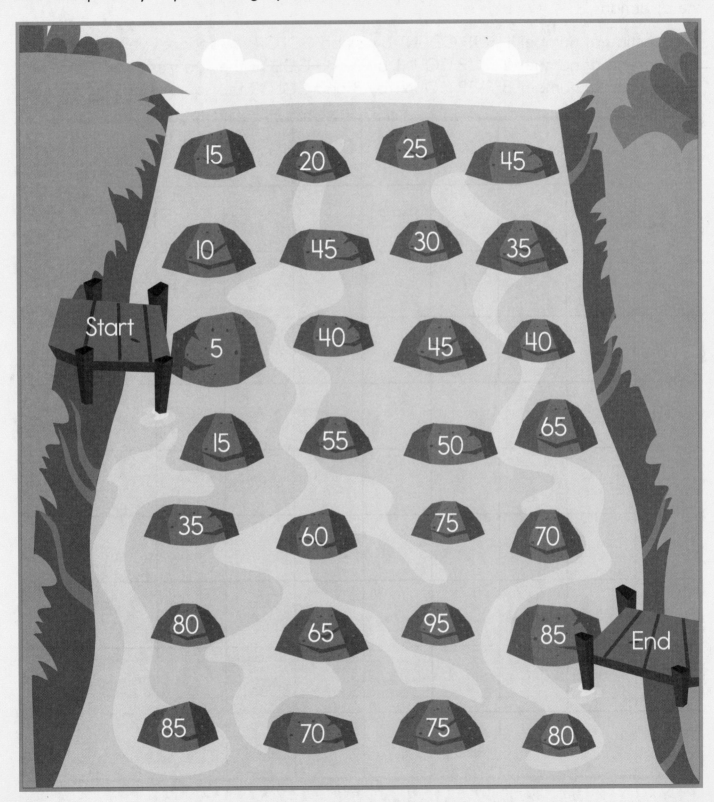

Three for Thrills

WRITE the numbers in the hundreds chart. Then COLOR the chart by following the directions.

1. Starting at number 1, SKIP COUNT by 3 and COLOR the squares yellow.
2. Starting at number 2, SKIP COUNT by 3 and COLOR the squares blue.
3. Starting at number 3, SKIP COUNT by 3 and COLOR the squares orange.

1	2								10
11									20
21									30
31									40
41									50
51									60
61									70
71									80
81									90
91									100

2

Skip to My Loo

SKIP COUNT by 10, 4, and 7, and WRITE the numbers along each track.

Skip count by:

10	4	7
10	4	7
20		

Finish

Just Right

WRITE each number next to a smaller blue number.

HINT: There may be more than one place to put a number, but you need to use every number.

742	113	981	187	256	677	409	556	823	399

599

98

1

2

724

545

3

4

750

251

5

6

830

400

7

8

178

398

9

10

Totally Tangled

Each numbered circle is connected to another numbered circle. FIND the pairs of numbers, and COLOR the circle with the smaller number.

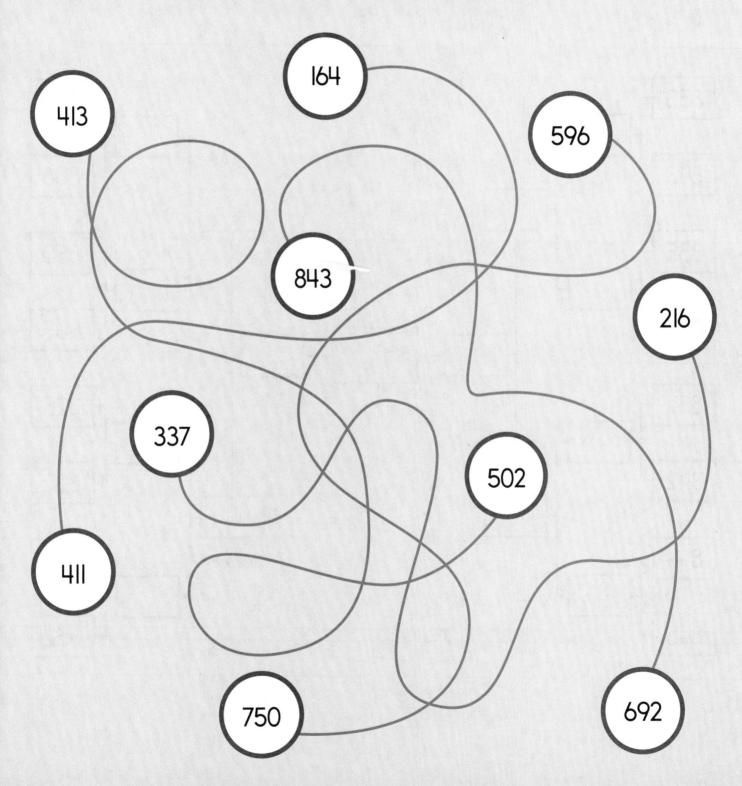

Win Big

Wherever two boxes point to one box, WRITE the larger number. Start at the sides and work toward the center to see which number will win big.

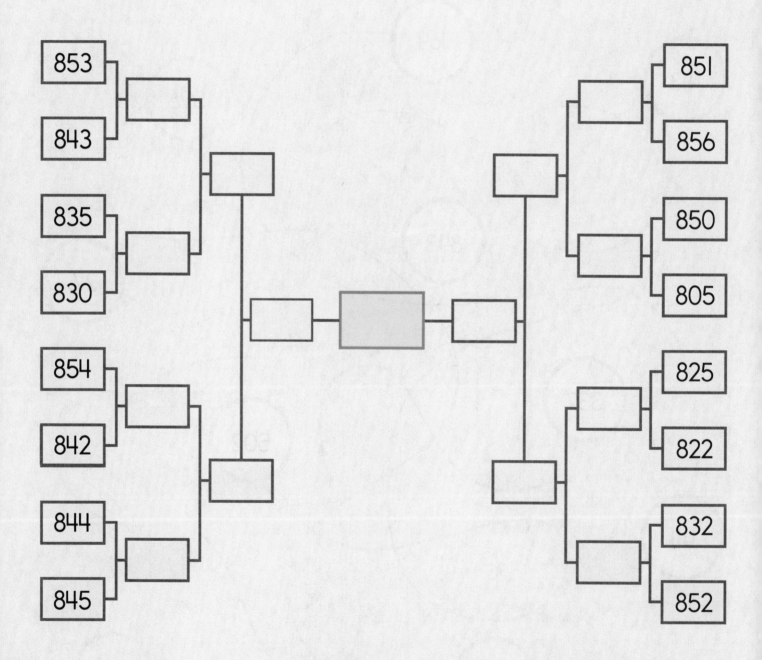

Roll It

ROLL a number cube, and WRITE the number in the first box. ROLL the number cube two more times, and WRITE the numbers in the second and third boxes. Then ROUND each number to the nearest ten and the nearest hundred.

HINT: Numbers that end in 1 through 49 get rounded down to the nearest hundred, and numbers that end in 50 through 99 get rounded up to the nearest hundred.

			Nearest Ten	Nearest Hundred

Rounding & Estimating

Just Right

WRITE each of the numbers to correctly complete the sentences. There may be more than one place to put a number, but you need to use every number.

HINT: Numbers that end in 1 through 49 get rounded down to the nearest hundred, and numbers that end in 50 through 99 get rounded up to the nearest hundred.

549	278	709	751	952
717	932	285	544	

1. _____ rounded to the nearest hundred is 300.

2. _____ rounded to the nearest ten is 540.

3. _____ rounded to the nearest hundred is 700.

4. _____ rounded to the nearest ten is 950.

5. _____ rounded to the nearest hundred is 500.

6. _____ rounded to the nearest ten is 280.

7. _____ rounded to the nearest hundred is 900.

8. _____ rounded to the nearest ten is 720.

9. _____ rounded to the nearest hundred is 800.

Fitting In

GUESS how many marbles are needed to fill the circle. WRITE your guess. Then turn the page to CHECK your guess.

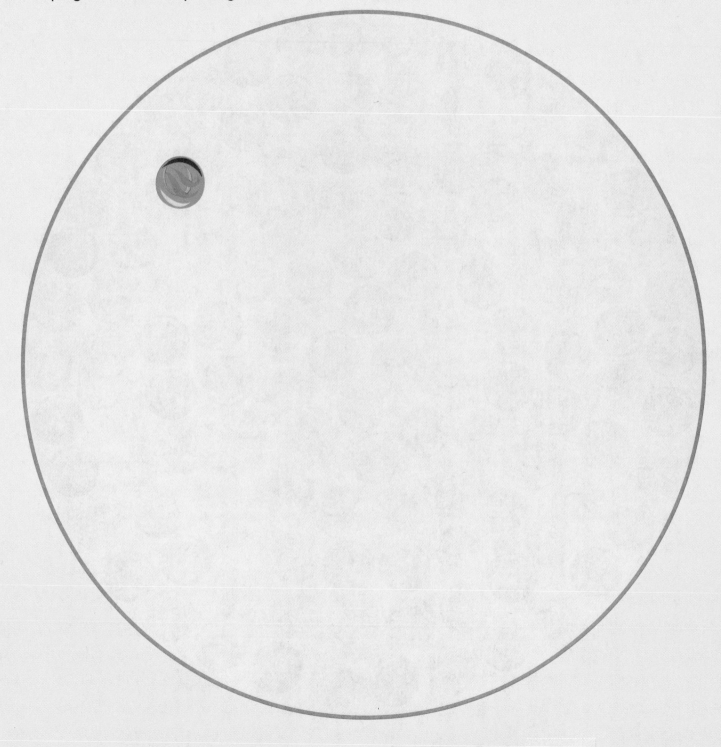

Guess: marbles

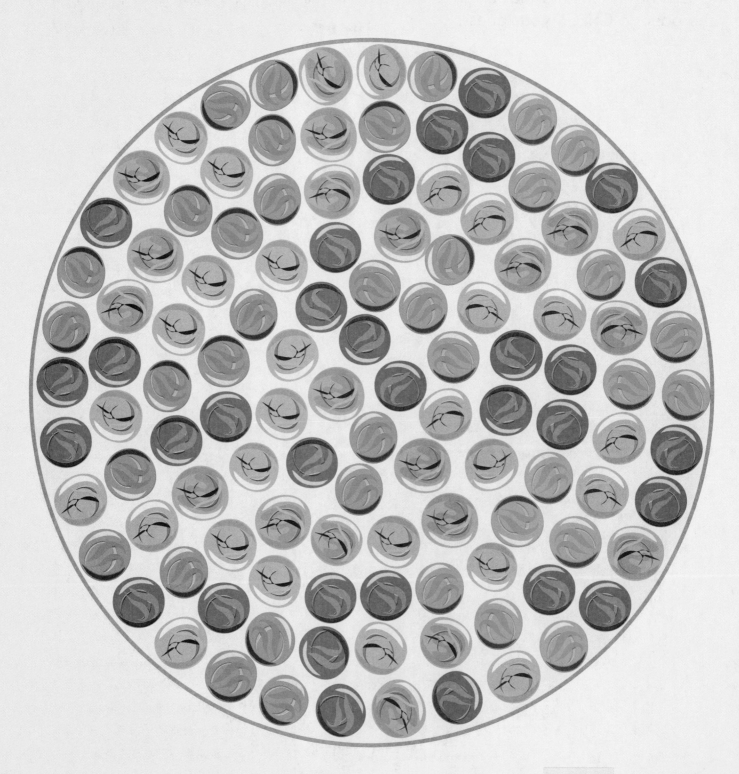

Check: [   ] marbles

Fitting In

GUESS how many pennies are needed to fill the square. WRITE your guess. Then fill the square with pennies to CHECK your guess.

Guess: _____ pennies   Check: _____ pennies

Missing Middles

WRITE the number missing from the center square.

1.
```
        32
        +
17  +       =  38
        =
        53
```

2.
```
        43
        +
50  +       =  66
        =
        59
```

3.
```
        12
        +
44  +       =  89
        =
        57
```

4.
```
        20
        +
41  +       =  78
        =
        57
```

5.
```
        31
        +
23  +       =  85
        =
        93
```

6.
```
        45
        +
16  +       =  70
        =
        99
```

Crossing Paths

WRITE the missing numbers.

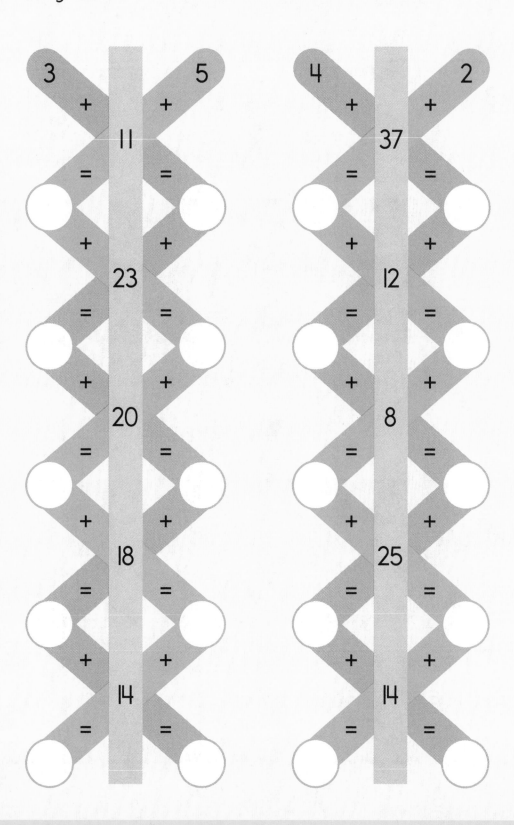

Super Square

WRITE numbers in the empty squares to finish all of the addition problems.

3	+	12	=	
+		+		+
9	+		=	
=		=		=
	+	37	=	

Code Breaker

SOLVE each problem. WRITE the letter that matches each sum to solve the riddle.

```
    11          38          46          21
  + 26        + 30        + 13        + 58
  _____      _____      _____      _____
  1           2           3           4
    O           L           V           C

    43          17          81          67
  + 52        + 31        + 12        + 10
  _____      _____      _____      _____
  5           6           7           8
    P           I           N           A

    29          13          62          77
  + 34        + 58        + 18        + 14
  _____      _____      _____      _____
  9           10          11          12
    T           G           E           S
```

Where does the pencil go on vacation?

___ ___   ___ ___ ___ ___   ___ ___
48 63   71 37 80 91   63 37

___ ___ ___ ___ ___ ___ ___ ___ ___ ___ ___ .
95 80 93 79 48 68 59 77 93 48 77

125

Pipe Down

WRITE each number. Then FOLLOW the pipe, and WRITE the same number in the next problem.

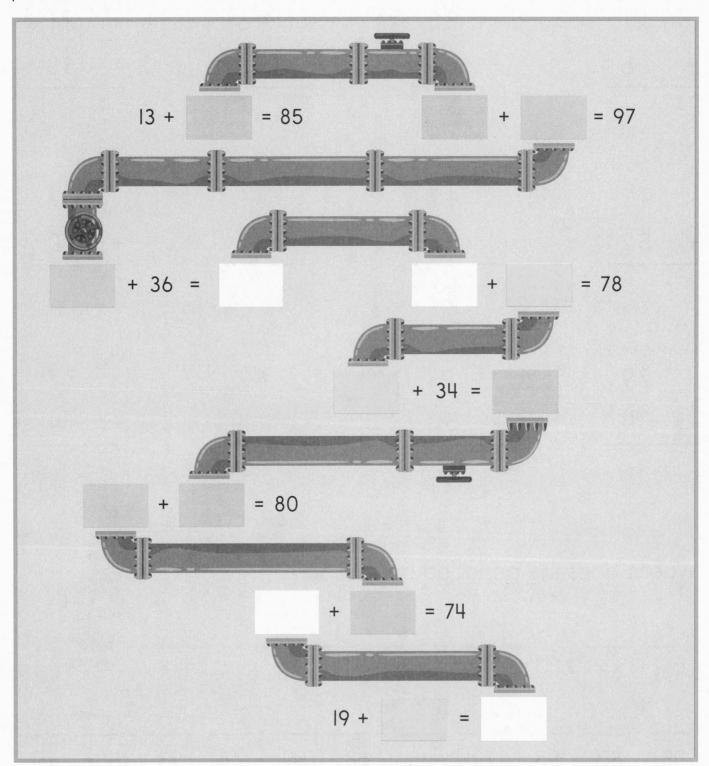

13 + ▢ = 85   ▢ + ▢ = 97

▢ + 36 = ▢   ▢ + ▢ = 78

+ 34 = ▢

▢ + ▢ = 80

▢ + ▢ = 74

19 + ▢ = ▢

Ground Floor

DRAW a line connecting one of the numbers in the windows at the top with the sum on the ground floor. CHOOSE one operation from each floor on the way down.

HINT: When you're done, can you find more ways to the ground floor?

Adding & Subtracting

Missing Middles

WRITE the number missing from the center square.

1.

```
        48
        –
25  –   [ ]  =  13
        =
        36
```

2.

```
        37
        –
78  –   [ ]  =  45
        =
        4
```

3.

```
        86
        –
99  –   [ ]  =  28
        =
        15
```

4.

```
        68
        –
59  –   [ ]  =  11
        =
        20
```

5.

```
        95
        –
44  –   [ ]  =  22
        =
        73
```

6.

```
        79
        –
58  –   [ ]  =  2
        =
        23
```

Crossing Paths

WRITE the missing numbers.

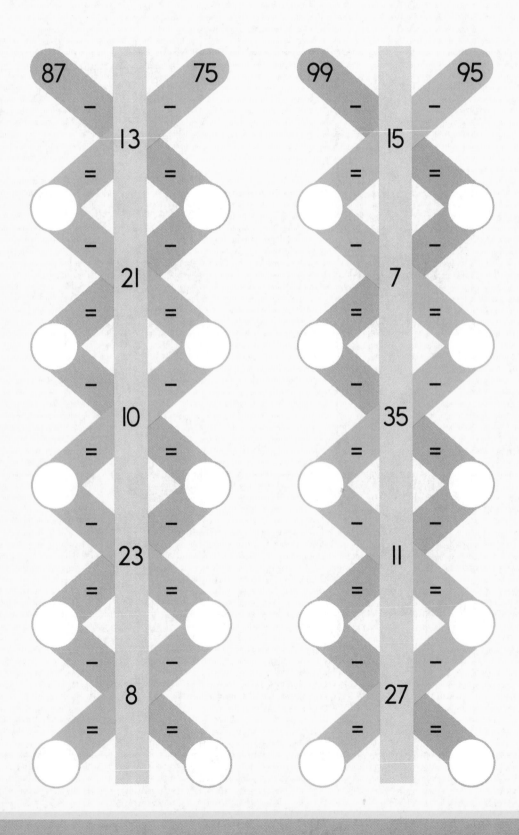

Adding & Subtracting

Super Square

WRITE numbers in the empty squares to finish all of the subtraction problems.

95	–		=	32
–		–		–
47	–		=	
=		=		=
	–	46	=	

Code Breaker

SOLVE each problem. WRITE the letter that matches each difference to solve the riddle.

42	75	18	84	91	72
− 11	− 52	− 16	− 62	− 45	− 23
1	2	3	4	5	6
W	D	O	A	L	V

63	71	72	96	60	52
− 37	− 19	− 59	− 49	− 24	− 36
7	8	9	10	11	12
U	T	S	Y	E	H

If you took two toys away from seven toys, how many toys would you have?

___	___	___		___	___	___	___
47	2	26		31	2	26	46	23

___	___	___	___		___	___	___
16	22	49	36		52	31	2

___	___	___	___
52	2	47	13

Pipe Down

WRITE each number. Then FOLLOW the pipe, and WRITE the same number in the next problem.

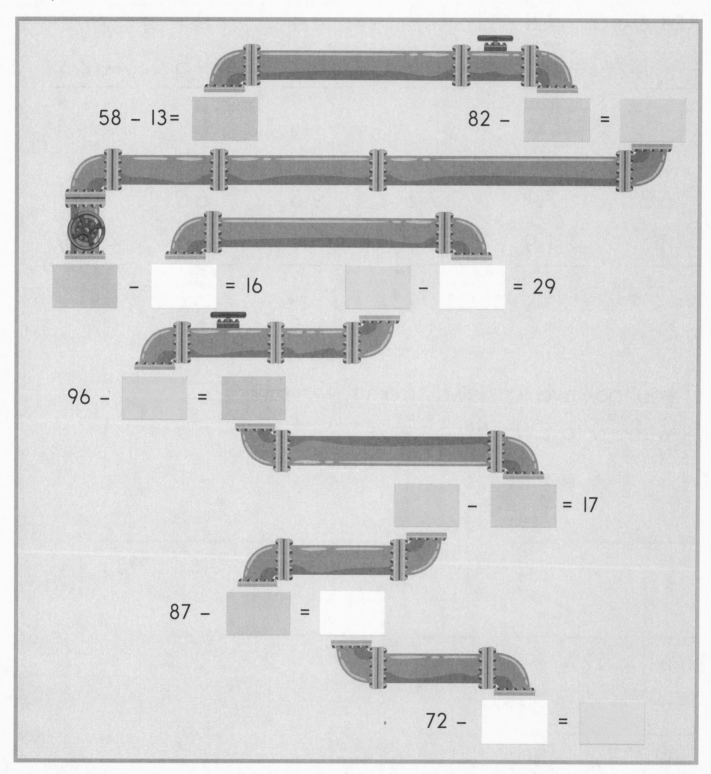

58 – 13 = ☐   82 – ☐ = ☐

☐ – ☐ = 16   ☐ – ☐ = 29

96 – ☐ = ☐

☐ – ☐ = 17

87 – ☐ = ☐

72 – ☐ = ☐

Ground Floor

DRAW a line connecting one of the numbers in the windows at the top with the difference on the ground floor. CHOOSE one operation from each floor on the way down.

HINT: When you're done, can you find more ways to the ground floor?

Sandy Shore

DRAW two straight lines in the sand to create four equal sets of shells.

Car Clubs

FIND each kind of car in the picture. WRITE the number of groups that can be made from each kind of car.

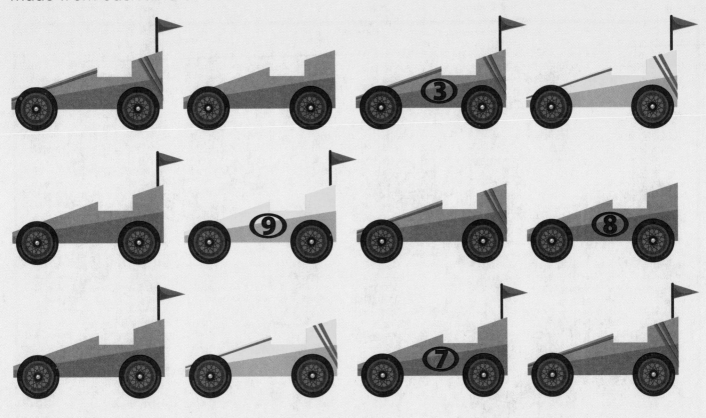

1. Groups of three blue cars ____3____

2. Groups of two cars with numbers _____

3. Groups of two cars with black wheels _____

4. Groups of four cars with flags _____

5. Groups of three yellow cars _____

6. Groups of two cars with red stripes _____

Sandy Shore

DRAW three straight lines in the sand to create six equal sets of shells.

Bug Buddies

FIND each kind of bug in the picture. WRITE the number of groups that can be made from each kind of bug.

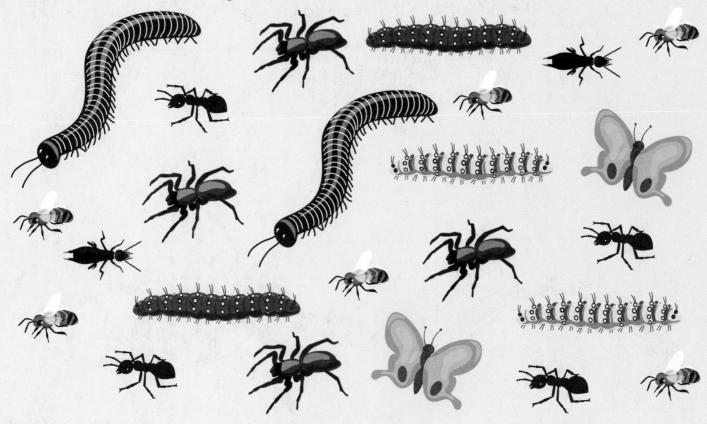

1. Groups of four brown bugs _____

2. Groups of two bugs with wings _____

3. Groups of three bugs with more than eight legs _____

4. Groups of two striped bugs _____

5. Groups of four bugs that can't fly _____

6. Groups of two bugs with eight legs _____

Bean Counter

Use the beans from page 197, and SHARE them equally among the bowls. Start with the number of beans listed, then WRITE how many beans will be in each bowl when the beans are shared equally. (Save the beans to use again later in the workbook.)

1. 9 beans: _____ per bowl

2. 15 beans: _____ per bowl

3. 6 beans: _____ per bowl

4. 18 beans: _____ per bowl

5. 24 beans: _____ per bowl

6. 12 beans: _____ per bowl

Going Bananas

The monkeys want bananas! DRAW a line from each monkey at the top to his basket at the bottom to collect the bananas. You can only cross each banana once, and the monkeys must each end up with the same number of bananas. You must use all of the bananas.

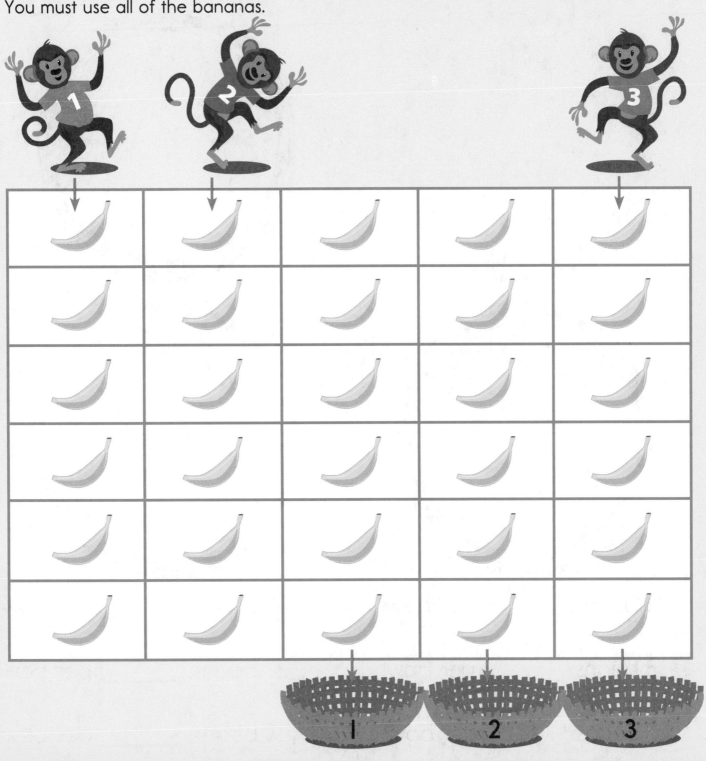

Bean Counter

Use the beans from page 197, and SHARE them equally among the bowls. Start with the number of beans listed, then WRITE how many beans will be in each bowl when the beans are shared equally. (Save the beans to use again.)

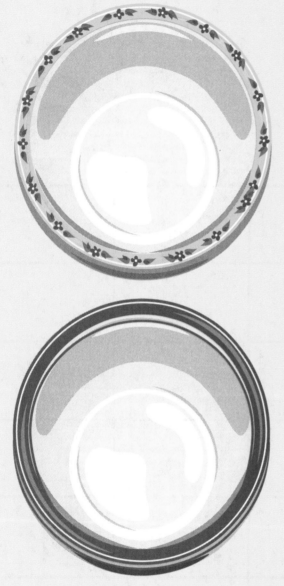

1. 16 beans: _____ per bowl   2. 32 beans: _____ per bowl

3. 8 beans: _____ per bowl   4. 28 beans: _____ per bowl

5. 20 beans: _____ per bowl   6. 48 beans: _____ per bowl

Count and Capture

The object of the game is to capture the most beans. Use the beans from page 197, an egg carton with the top cut off, and two small bowls. READ the rules. PLAY the game.

1. Set up the game by putting the bowls at either end of the egg carton and placing four beans in each egg carton section. Each player owns the sections on his side.

2. The youngest player goes first. To take a turn, a player scoops up all of the beans from one of his sections, then places one bean at a time in each section, moving to the right (counterclockwise).

   Example: Player 1 scoops up four beans from the yellow section, and places one bean in each orange section that follows to the right.

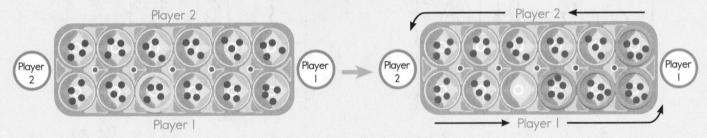

3. A player captures beans when placing a bean in any of the other player's sections to make a total of two or three beans. Captured beans go in the player's bowl.

   Example: Player 1 moves the beans from the yellow section and captures the beans in the two orange sections because the total number of beans is two and three. He then puts all of the captured beans in his bowl.

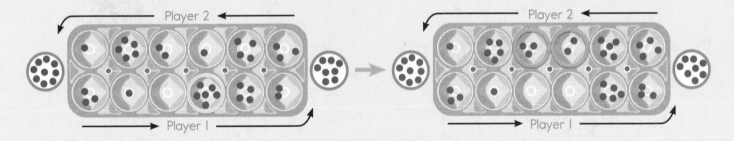

4. Play continues until all of the beans are captured or no more moves can be made.

The player with the most beans wins!

Code Breaker

FIND the odd or even number in each row. Then WRITE the letter that matches each number to solve the riddle.

FIND the odd number in each row.

1.	3	4	8	K
2.	10	7	6	W
3.	2	9	14	A
4.	8	12	1	H

FIND the even number in each row.

5.	7	5	6	E
6.	12	9	11	T
7.	8	15	3	Y
8.	1	10	13	S

How do you make seven even?

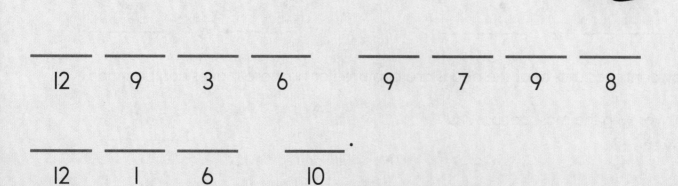

___ ___ ___ ___   ___ ___ ___ ___
12   9   3   6   9   7   9   8

___ ___ ___   ___ .
12   1   6   10

Odd Way Out

START at the arrow. DRAW a line through only odd numbers to get to the smiley face.

Where's My Brain?

START at the arrow. DRAW a path through only even numbers to reach the brain.

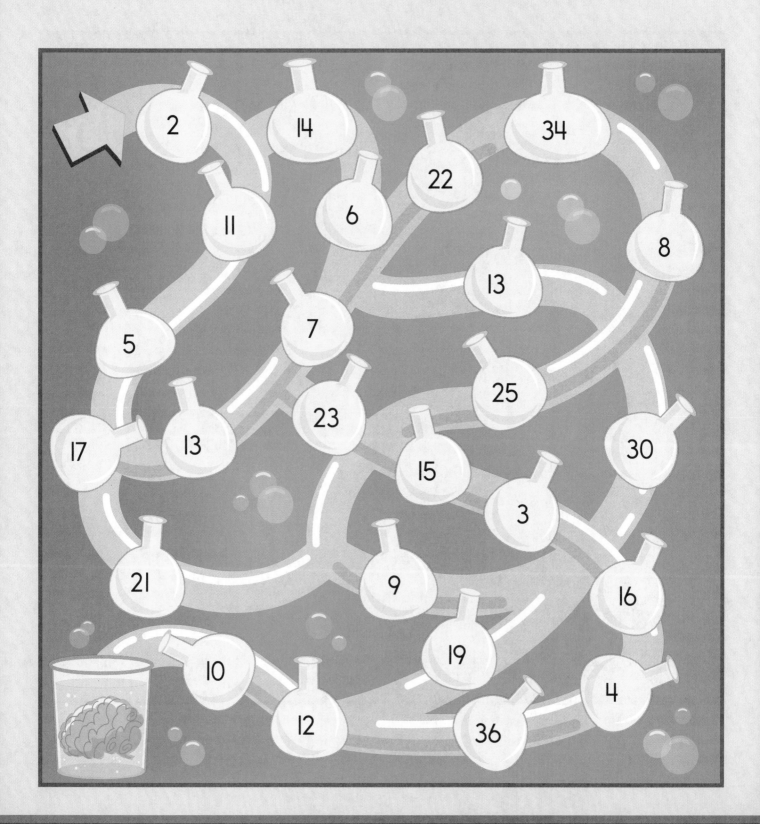

Alien Adventure

Can you be the first alien to reach the spaceship? Use two small objects as playing pieces and the spinner from page 199. READ the rules. PLAY the game! (Save the spinner to use again later in the workbook.)

Rules: Two players
1. Place the playing pieces at Start.
2. Take turns spinning the spinner. If you spin Odd, move to the next odd number. If you spin Even, move to the next even number.
3. If you land on a space with an asteroid, you lose a turn.

The first player to get to the spaceship wins!

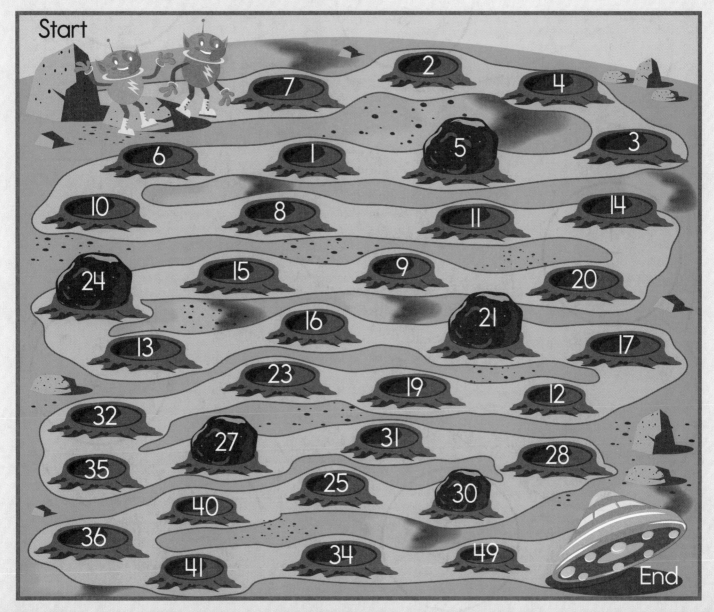

Totally Tangled

FIND the fraction and picture pairs that are connected, and COLOR any fraction that does **not** match the picture.

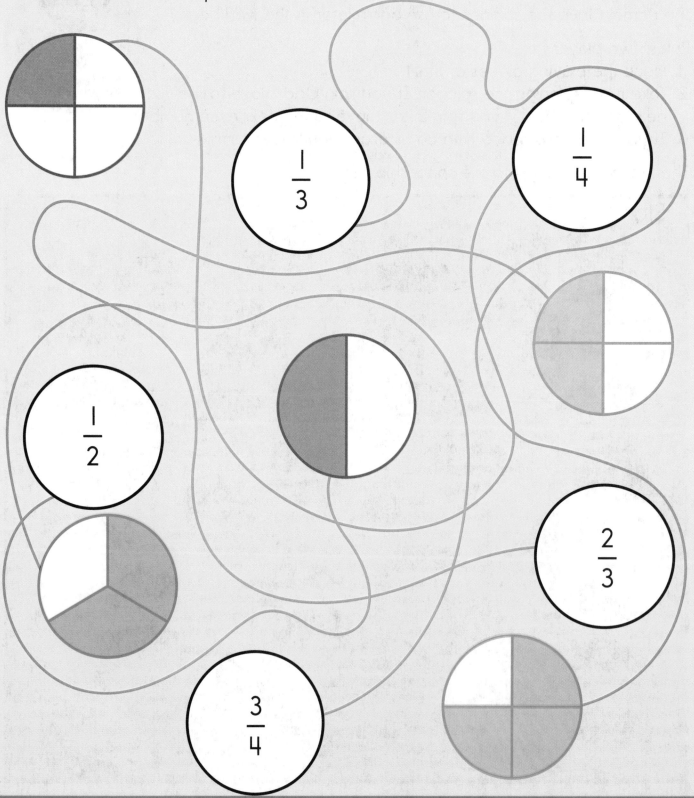

8

Make a Match

CUT OUT the fractions and pictures. READ the rules. PLAY the game!

Rules: Two players
1. Place the cards face down on a table.
2. Take turns turning over two cards at a time.
3. Keep the cards when you match a fraction and a picture that shows that fraction shaded.

The player with the most matches wins!

$\frac{1}{4}$		$\frac{1}{3}$	
$\frac{1}{2}$		$\frac{2}{3}$	
$\frac{2}{2}$		$\frac{3}{4}$	

Mystery Picture

COLOR each section according to the fractions to reveal the mystery picture.

Fractions

Fraction Factory

Can you be the first to reach the end? Use two small objects as playing pieces and the spinner from page 200. READ the rules. PLAY the game!

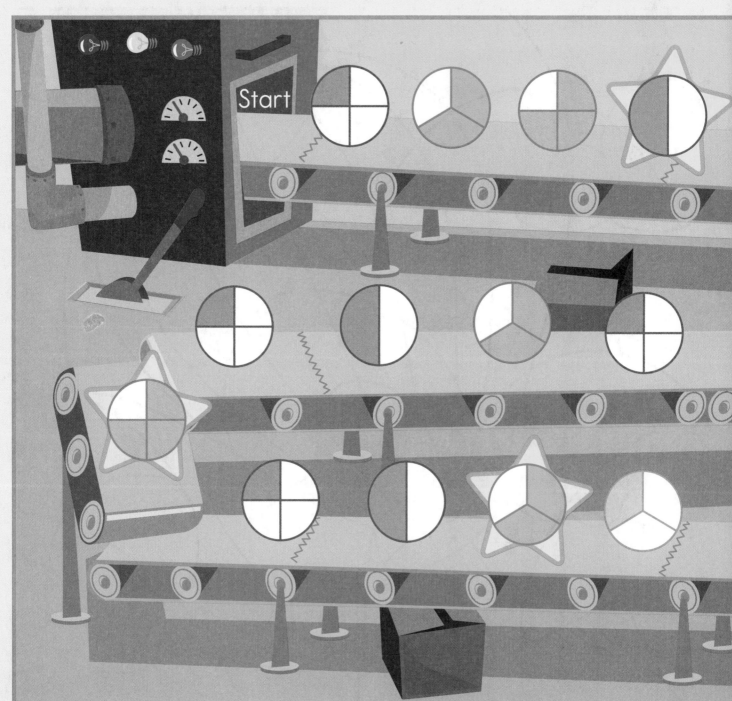

Rules: Two players
1. Place the playing pieces at Start.
2. Take turns spinning the spinner. Move to the closest fraction picture that matches the fraction on the spinner.
3. If you land on a space with a star, you get to spin again.

The first player to get to the End box wins!

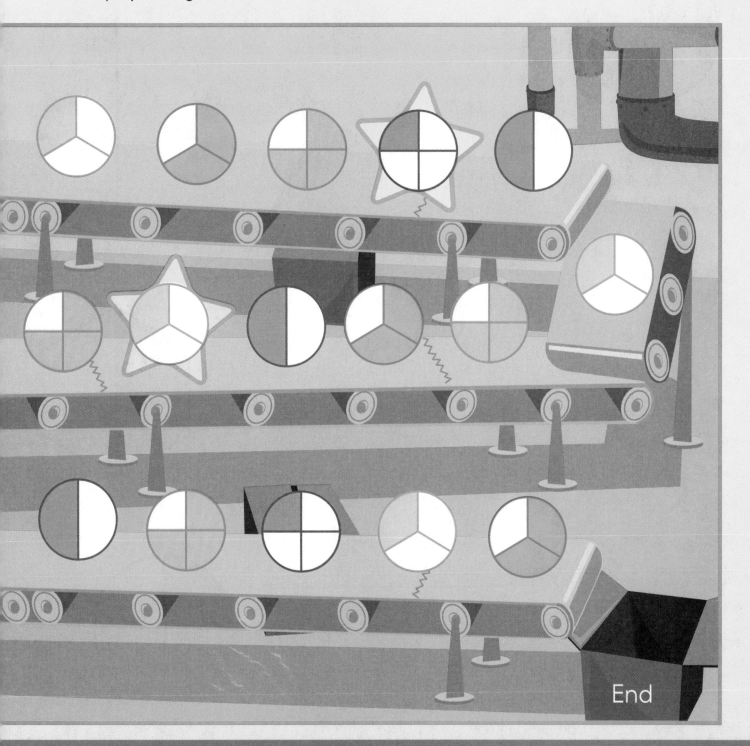

Picking Pairs

DRAW a line to connect each equivalent pair of fraction pictures.

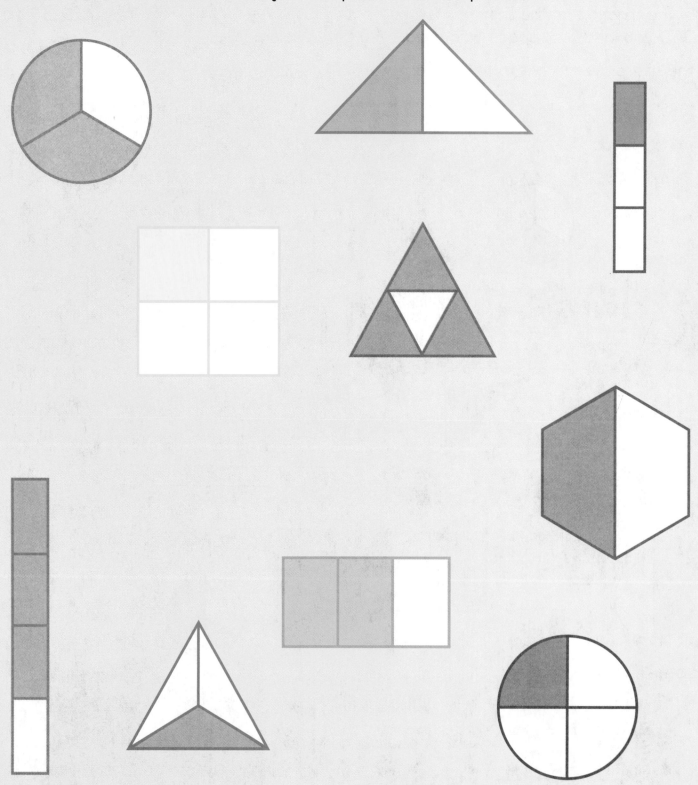

Totally Tangled

Each fraction is connected to another fraction. FIND the pairs of fractions, and COLOR the circle with the larger fraction.

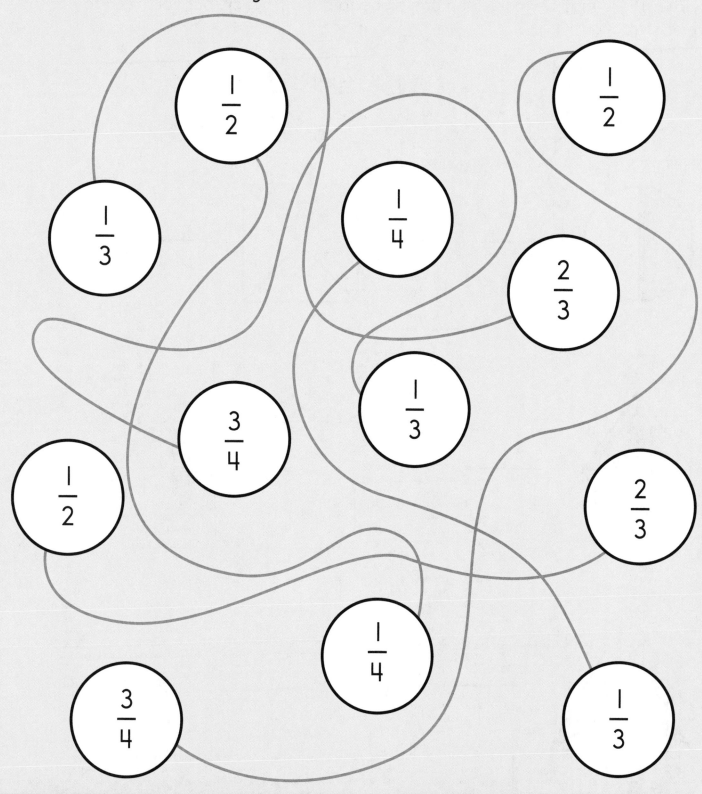

Just Right

WRITE each of these fractions next to a smaller fraction picture.

HINT: There may be more than one place to put a fraction, but you need to use every fraction.

$$\frac{1}{3} \qquad \frac{3}{4} \qquad \frac{2}{3} \qquad \frac{1}{2} \qquad \frac{4}{4}$$

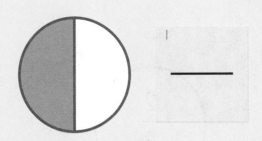

1 _____

2 _____

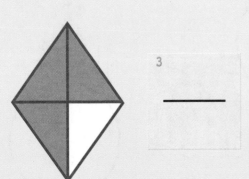

3 _____

4 _____

5 _____

Code Breaker

CIRCLE the larger fraction in each pair. Then WRITE the letter that matches each fraction to solve the riddle.

1 $\frac{1}{4}$ $\frac{1}{3}$	2 $\frac{3}{4}$ $\frac{2}{4}$	3 $\frac{1}{2}$ $\frac{2}{2}$	4 $\frac{1}{2}$ $\frac{1}{3}$
W	E	T	O

5 $\frac{2}{4}$ $\frac{1}{3}$	6 $\frac{3}{3}$ $\frac{1}{2}$	7 $\frac{2}{4}$ $\frac{2}{3}$	8 $\frac{4}{4}$ $\frac{2}{3}$
L	H	I	N

Why did the boat carrying three thirds sink?

There was a ___ ___ ___ ___ ___
        $\frac{1}{3}$ $\frac{3}{3}$ $\frac{1}{2}$ $\frac{2}{4}$ $\frac{3}{4}$

___ ___ ___ ___.
$\frac{2}{3}$ $\frac{4}{4}$ $\frac{2}{3}$ $\frac{2}{2}$

Hidden Shapes

FIND each shape hidden in the picture. DRAW a line to connect each shape with its location in the picture.

HINT: Be sure to use shapes that match in size.

Doodle Pad

TRACE the shapes. Then DRAW a picture using each shape.

Shape Shifters

A shape has **symmetry** if a line can divide the shape so each half is a mirror image of the other. Use the pattern block pieces from page 201, and PLACE the pieces to make each picture symmetrical without overlapping any pieces. (Save the pattern block pieces to use again later in the workbook.)

Cool Kaleidoscope

COLOR the kaleidoscope so it is symmetrical.

HINT: Make a mirror image across each line.

Shape Shifters

Use the pattern block pieces from page 201, and PLACE the pieces to completely fill each shape without overlapping any pieces. See if you can solve the puzzles different ways. (Save the pattern block pieces to use again.)

Puzzling Pentominoes

Perimeter is the distance around a two-dimensional shape. Use the pentomino pieces from page 203, and PLACE the pieces to completely fill each shape without overlapping any pieces. Then WRITE the perimeter of each shape. (Save the pentomino pieces to use again.)

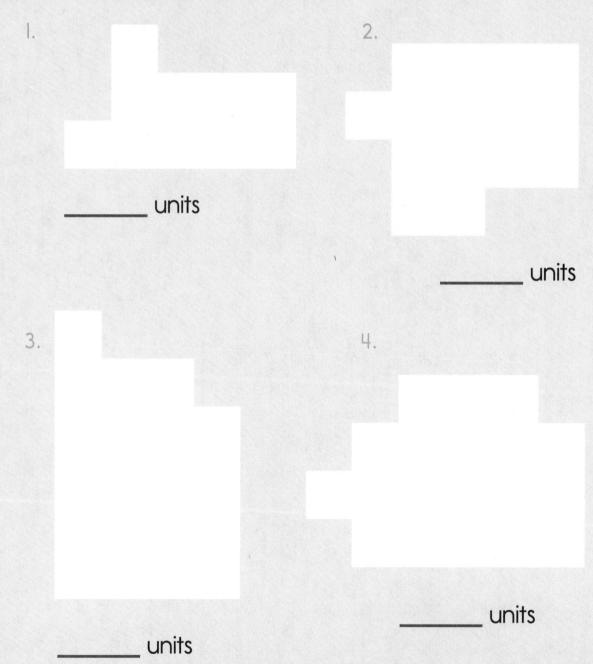

1.

_____ units

2.

_____ units

3.

_____ units

4.

_____ units

Shape Creator

DRAW six different shapes that all have a perimeter of 12 units.

Puzzling Pentominoes

Area is the size of the surface of a shape, and it is measured in square units. Use the pentomino pieces from page 203, and PLACE the pieces to completely fill each shape without overlapping any pieces. Then WRITE the area of each shape.

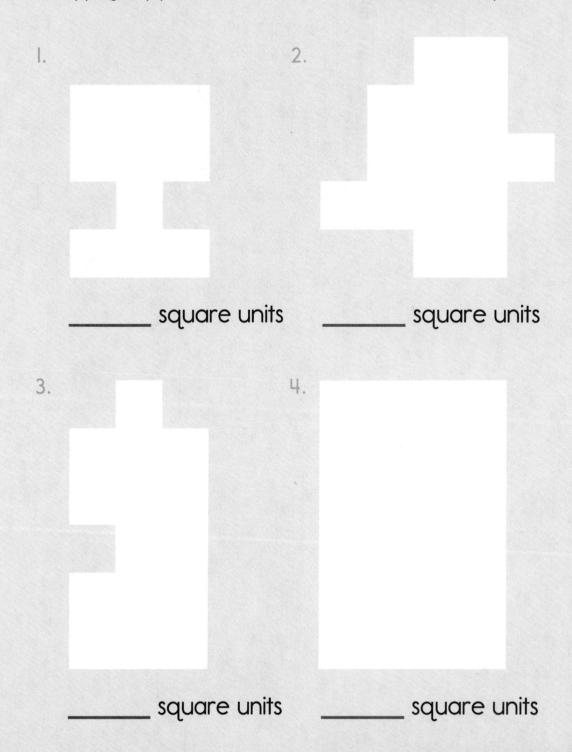

1.

_____ square units

2.

_____ square units

3.

_____ square units

4.

_____ square units

Shape Creator

DRAW six different shapes that all have an area of 10 square units.

Animal Adventure

WRITE the name of the animal that can be found at each location on the map.

HINT: Follow the letter and the number and see where the two lines meet.

1. C5 _____

2. C1 _____

3. E1 _____

4. D3 _____

5. A6 _____

6. A4 _____

7. C7 _____

8. B2 _____

9. E5 _____

10. E7 _____

Treasure Hunt

Use the squares on the map to find the pirate treasure. FOLLOW the directions.
DRAW an X where the treasure is buried.

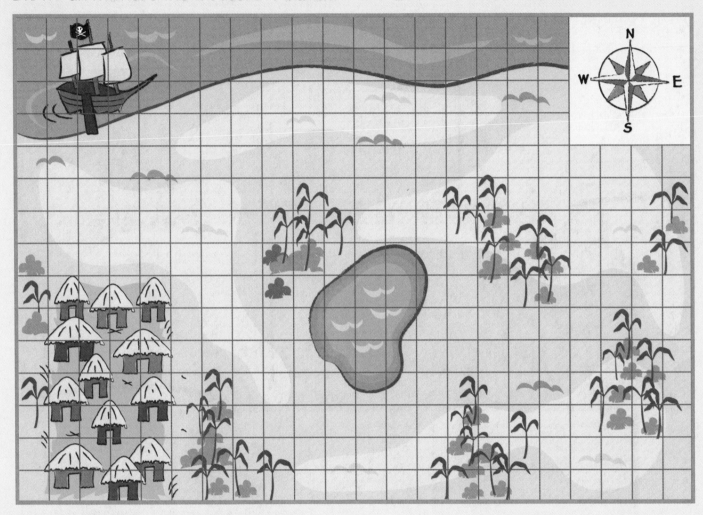

Blackbeard's Treasure

1. From the ship travel 4 squares south. Do not enter the village or the people will be curious.
2. Go 5 squares to the east, and turn to head 5 squares south.
3. Travel 6 squares to the east and 2 squares to the north to get around the lake.
4. Go another 5 squares east and you'll nearly be there.
5. Head 5 squares north. Can the treasure be near?
6. Go 2 squares west and draw an X. That's where the treasure will be!

Hamster Hotel

Each hamster is four coins long. MEASURE each hamster with a line of four quarters, dimes, nickels, and pennies. When you find a match, WRITE the coin name.

1. _____

2. _____

3. _____

4. _____

Sidewalk Slugs

LINE UP dimes and MEASURE each slug. DRAW lines connecting pairs of slugs that are about the same length.

Code Ruler

WRITE the letter that matches each measurement to answer the riddle.

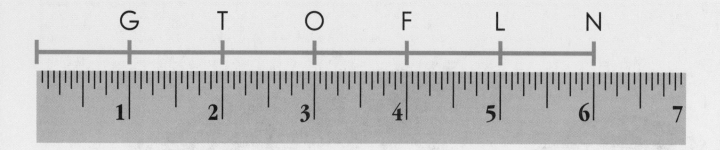

G   T   O   F   L   N

1   2   3   4   5   6   7

What is a ruler's favorite kind of hot dog?

A _____ _____ _____ _____ _____ _____ _____ _____ .

    4 in.   3 in.   3 in.   2 in.   5 in.   3 in.   6 in.   1 in.

Bowl of Candy

One pack of candy in the bowl is not the same length as the others. MEASURE each pack of candy in inches, and CIRCLE the one that is not the same length.

Code Ruler

WRITE the letter that matches each measurement to answer the riddle.

M N B E A I O P C R K S H W T

1 2 3 4 5 6 7 8 9 10 11 12 13 14 15 16

How do you measure a skunk?

___ ___   ___ ___ ___ ___   ___ ___ —
6 cm 2 cm   12 cm 9 cm 4 cm 2 cm   15 m 6 cm

___ ___ ___ ___ ___ ___ .
1 cm 4 cm 15 cm 4 cm 10 cm 12 cm

Pick a Pencil

One colored pencil is not the same length as the others. MEASURE each pencil in centimeters, and CIRCLE the one that is not the same length.

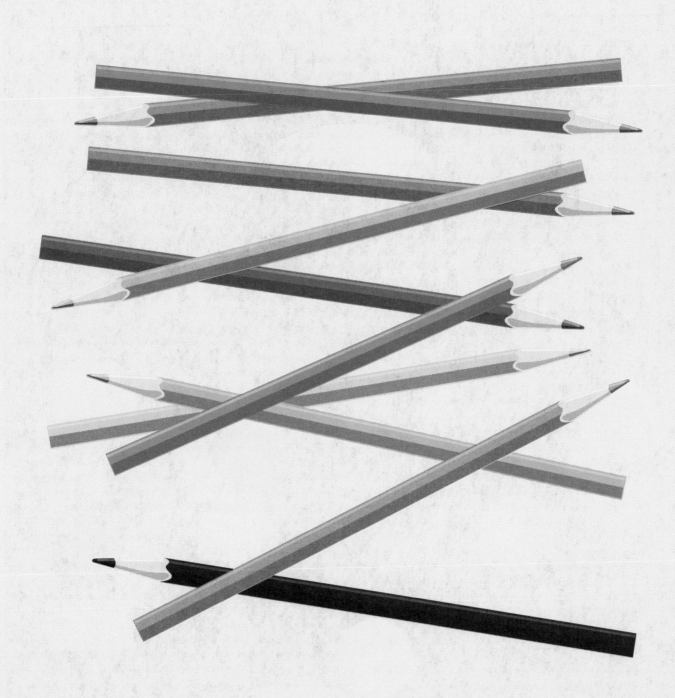

Minigolf

WRITE the numbers 1 through 6 on the golf balls so that 1 is the ball you think is closest to the hole and 6 is the golf ball you think is farthest away. Then MEASURE in inches to see if you're correct.

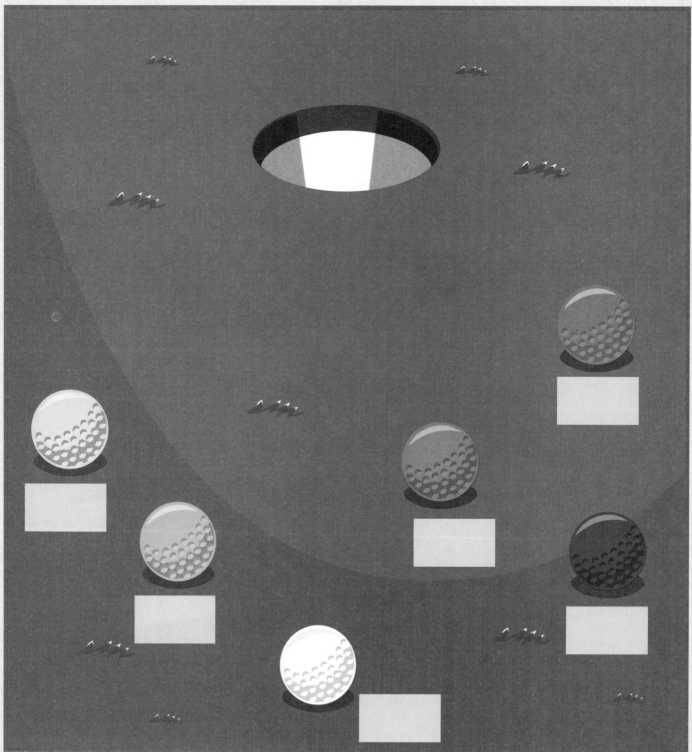

Don't Go Over

GUESS the height of each ice pop and stick in centimeters. Then MEASURE each ice pop. For every centimeter in the difference between the two measurements, COLOR a section in the white ice pop. If you get through the whole page without filling the ice pop, you win!

HINT: To find the difference, subtract the smaller measurement from the larger measurement.

Guess: _____

Check: _____

3

Guess: _____

Check: _____

Guess: _____

Check: _____

4

Guess: _____

Check: _____

1

Guess: _____

Check: _____

2

So Far Away

WRITE the numbers 1 through 8 next to the ants so that 1 is the ant you think is closest to the entrance of the anthill and 8 is the ant you think is farthest away. Then MEASURE in centimeters to see if you're correct.

HINT: Use the dots to help you measure.

Don't Go Over

GUESS the distance between each matching pair of marbles in centimeters. Then MEASURE the distance. For every centimeter in the difference between the two measurements, COLOR a section in the white marble. If you get through the whole page without filling the marble, you win!

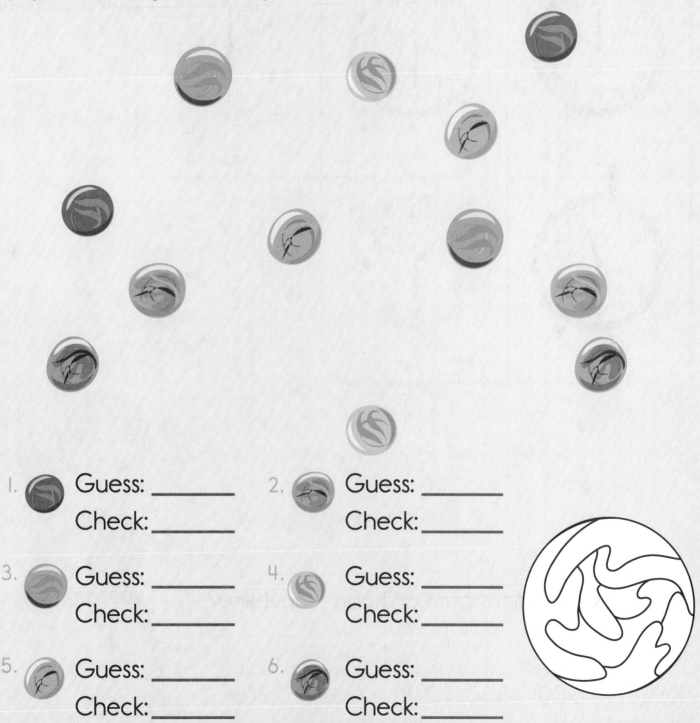

1. Guess: _____ Check: _____

2. Guess: _____ Check: _____

3. Guess: _____ Check: _____

4. Guess: _____ Check: _____

5. Guess: _____ Check: _____

6. Guess: _____ Check: _____

Code Breaker

WRITE the letter that matches each time to solve the riddle.

What has two hands but can't carry anything?

_____ _____ _____ _____ _____ _____ .

10:30   6:00   8:30   2:00   6:00   12:30

Mystery Time

COLOR the times in the picture according to the color of the clocks at the top. When you are done coloring, WRITE the mystery time under the picture.

Code Breaker

WRITE the letter that matches each time to solve the riddle.

| E | T | L |

| H | R |

Week Year Minute

What happens once in a year, twice in a week, and once in a minute?

_____ _____ _____
7:45   3:45   10:15

_____ _____ _____ _____ _____ _____ _____ .
2:15   10:15   7:45   7:45   10:15   8:15   10:15

Mystery Time

COLOR the times in the picture according to the color of the clocks at the top.
When you are done coloring, WRITE the mystery time under the picture.

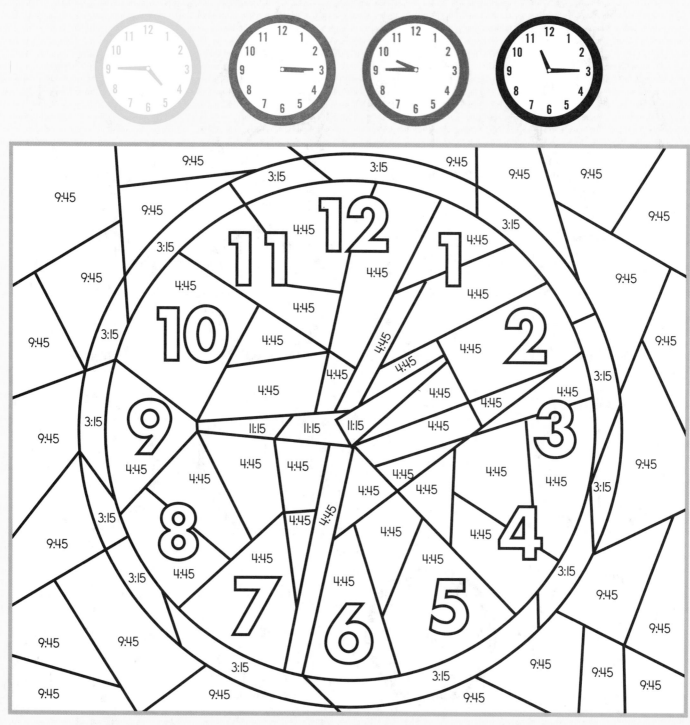

Adding & Subtracting Time

Time Travel

DRAW a line from Start through the clocks to get to the end, traveling
1 hour and 15 minutes ahead as you go from clock to clock.

Start

End

Time Travel

DRAW a line from Start through the clocks to get to the end, traveling
1 hour and 45 minutes back as you go from clock to clock.

Start

End

Adding & Subtracting Time

Code Breaker

WRITE the new time for each watch. Then WRITE the letter that matches each new time to solve the riddle.

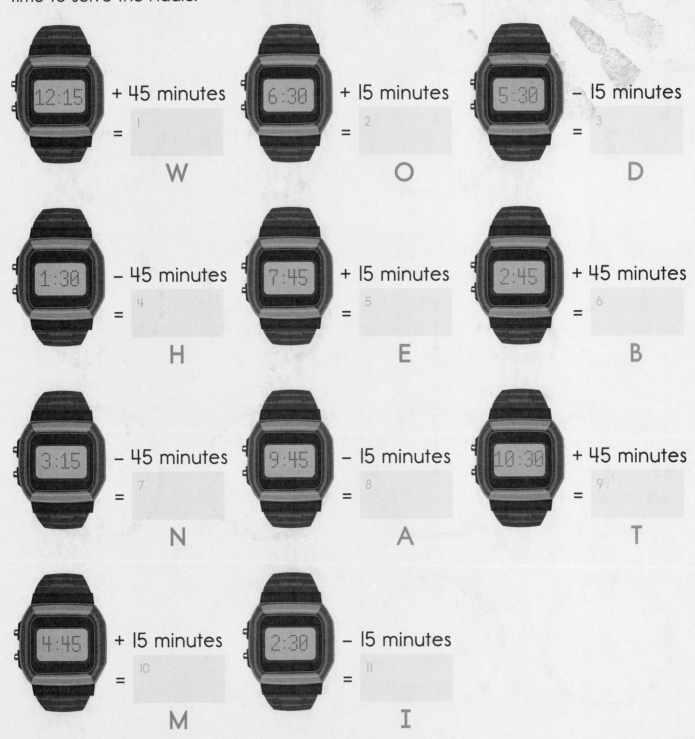

12:15 + 45 minutes
= 1 [____]
W

6:30 + 15 minutes
= 2 [____]
O

5:30 – 15 minutes
= 3 [____]
D

1:30 – 45 minutes
= 4 [____]
H

7:45 + 15 minutes
= 5 [____]
E

2:45 + 45 minutes
= 6 [____]
B

3:15 – 45 minutes
= 7 [____]
N

9:45 – 15 minutes
= 8 [____]
A

10:30 + 45 minutes
= 9 [____]
T

4:45 + 15 minutes
= 10 [____]
M

2:30 – 15 minutes
= 11 [____]
I

Why did the boy sit on the clock?

___ ___   ___ ___ ___ ___ ___ ___

12:45   8:00   1:00   9:30   2:30   11:15   8:00   5:15

___ ___   ___ ___   ___ ___

11:15   6:45   3:30   8:00   6:45   2:30

___ ___ ___ ___ .

11:15   2:15   5:00   8:00

Code Breaker

WRITE the value of each coin set. Then WRITE the letter that matches each value to solve the riddle.

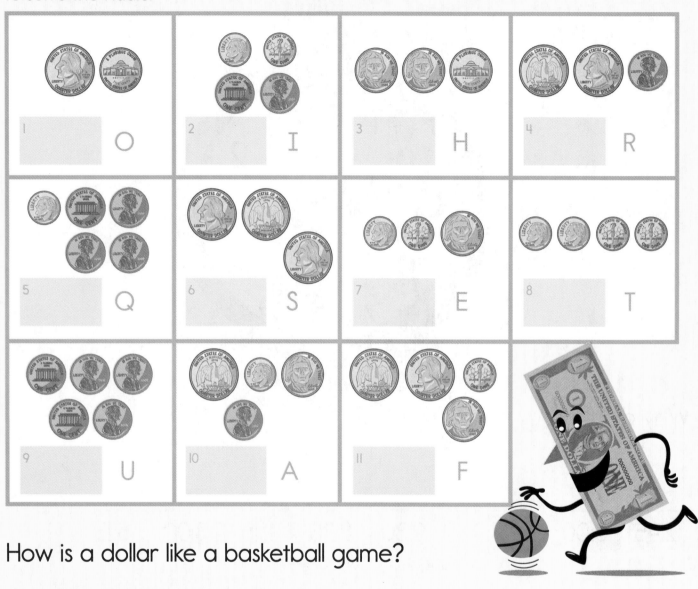

1 — O	2 — I	3 — H	4 — R
5 — Q	6 — S	7 — E	8 — T
9 — U	10 — A	11 — F	

How is a dollar like a basketball game?

___ ___ ___ ___ ___ ___ ___ ___ ___
22¢ 40¢   15¢ 41¢ 75¢   65¢ 30¢ 5¢ 51¢

___ ___ ___ ___ ___ ___ ___ ___ .
14¢ 5¢ 41¢ 51¢ 40¢ 25¢ 51¢ 75¢

Slide Sort

CIRCLE the dollar amounts that do **not** match the picture at the bottom of the slide.

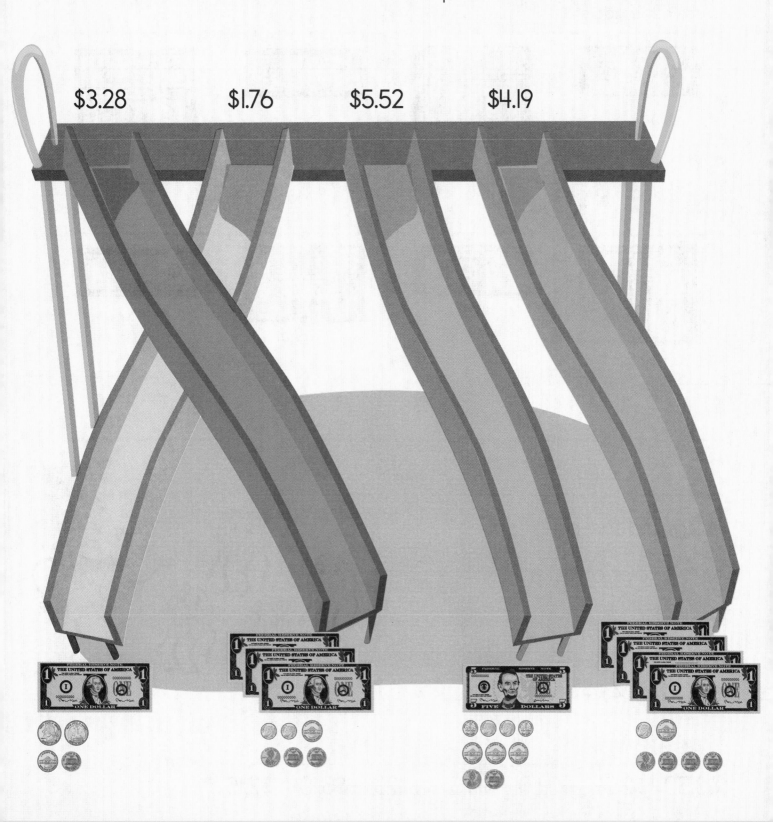

$3.28 $1.76 $5.52 $4.19

Code Breaker

WRITE the value of each money set. Then WRITE the letter that matches each value to solve the riddle.

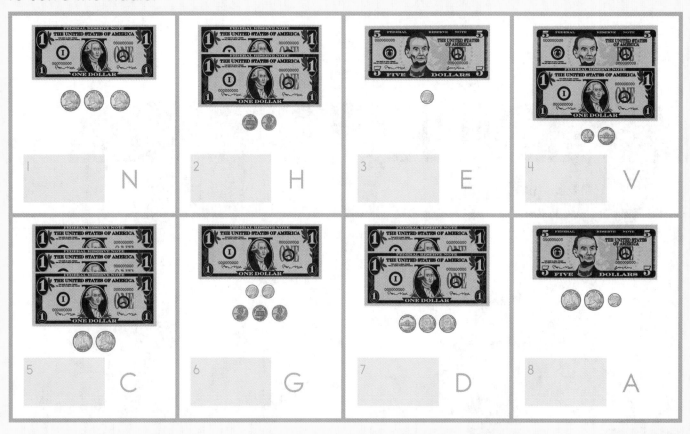

| 1   N | 2   H | 3   E | 4   V |
| 5   C | 6   G | 7   D | 8   A |

What did the dollar say

to the four quarters?

You ____ ____ ____ ____
    $2.02 $5.60 $6.15 $5.10

____ ____ ____ ____ ____ ____ ____ .
$3.50 $2.02 $5.60 $1.75 $1.23 $5.10 $2.15

Pocket Change

DRAW two straight lines to create four different money sets of equal value.

Pay the Price

CUT OUT the cards on pages 191 and 192. PLACE cards next to each price tag so that the cards total the same value. How many different ways can you place the cards for each price tag?

HINT: Use as many cards as you want, stacking them next to each price tag.

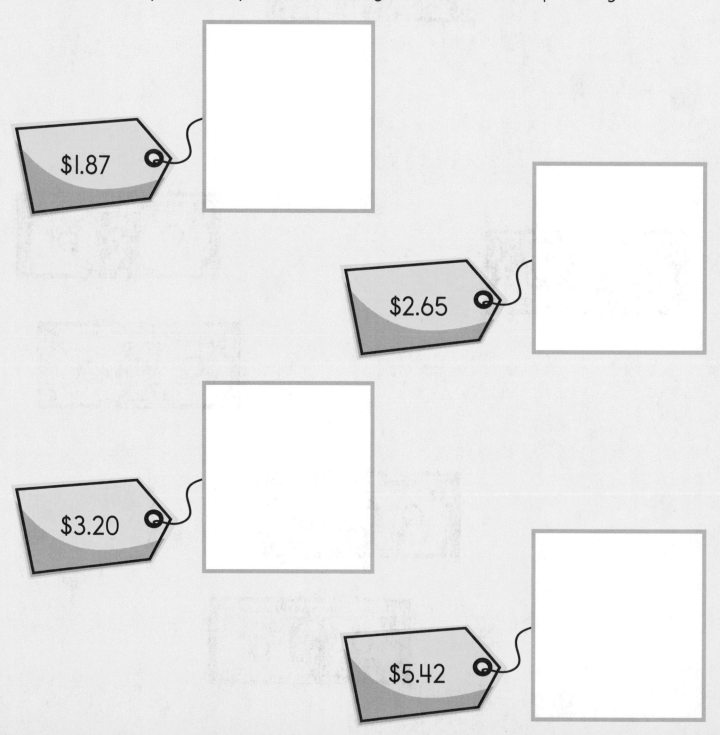

$1.87

$2.65

$3.20

$5.42

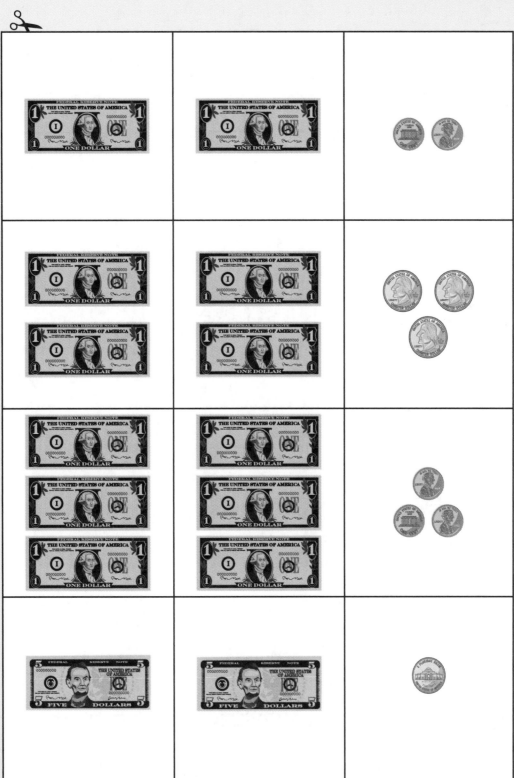

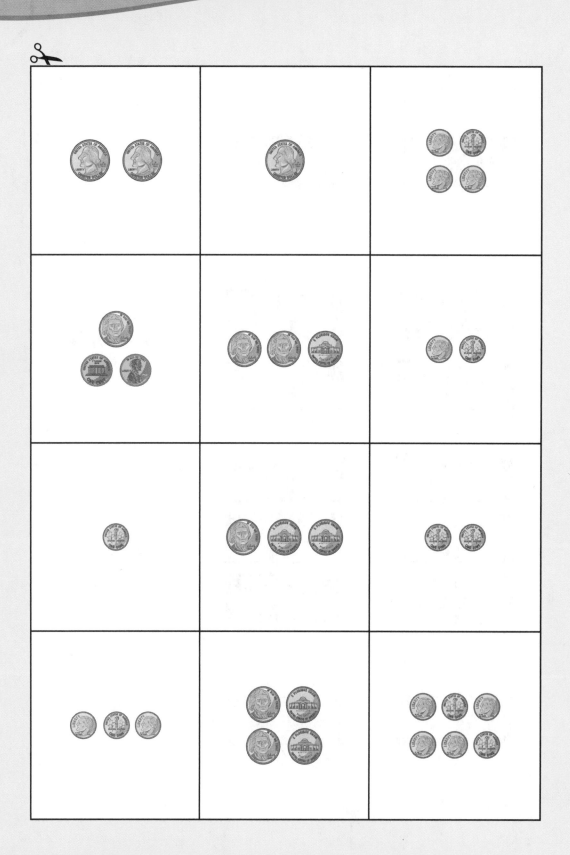

One Left Over

CROSS OUT all of the money that will be used to buy the items to reveal the extra coin.

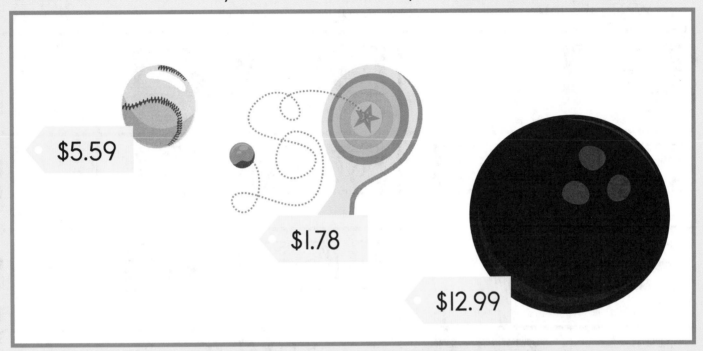

$5.59

$1.78

$12.99

Code Breaker

CIRCLE the picture in each row with less money than the other, and WRITE its value.
Then WRITE the letter that matches each value to solve the riddle.

What has a head and a tail but no body?

——— ——— ——— ——— ——— .
$3.07 $6.19 $1.50 $7.45 $4.98

Just Right

WRITE these dollar amounts so that each one is next to a picture with a smaller value.

HINT: There may be more than one place to put each amount, but you need to use every one.

| $2.29 | $4.98 | $5.14 | $1.03 | $6.37 |

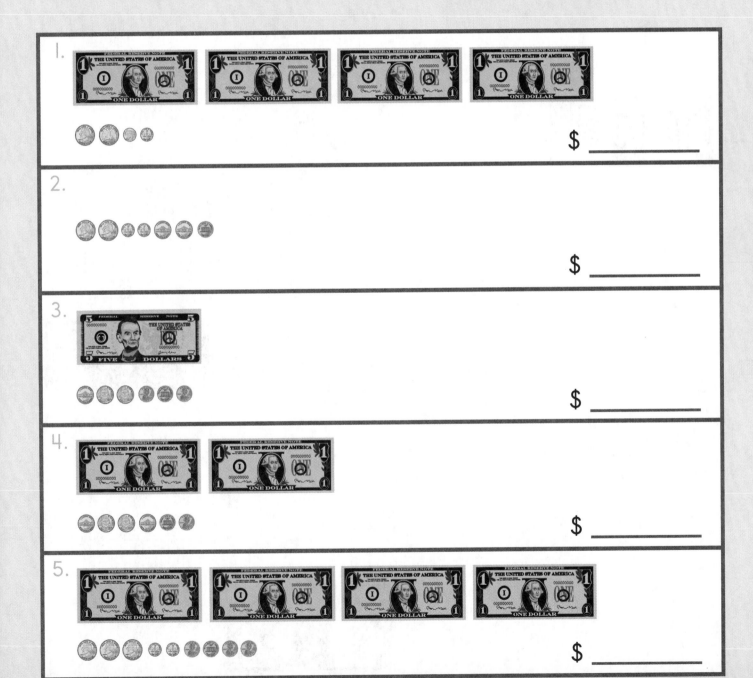

1. $ _____

2. $ _____

3. $ _____

4. $ _____

5. $ _____

Pocket Change

DRAW three straight lines to create six different money sets of equal value.

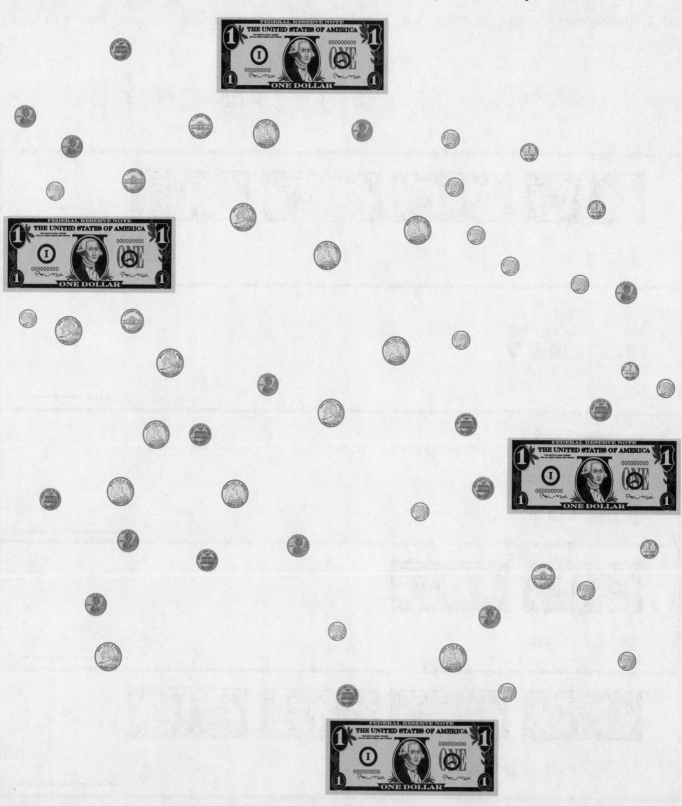

Beans

CUT OUT the beans.

These beans are for use with pages 138, 140, and 141.

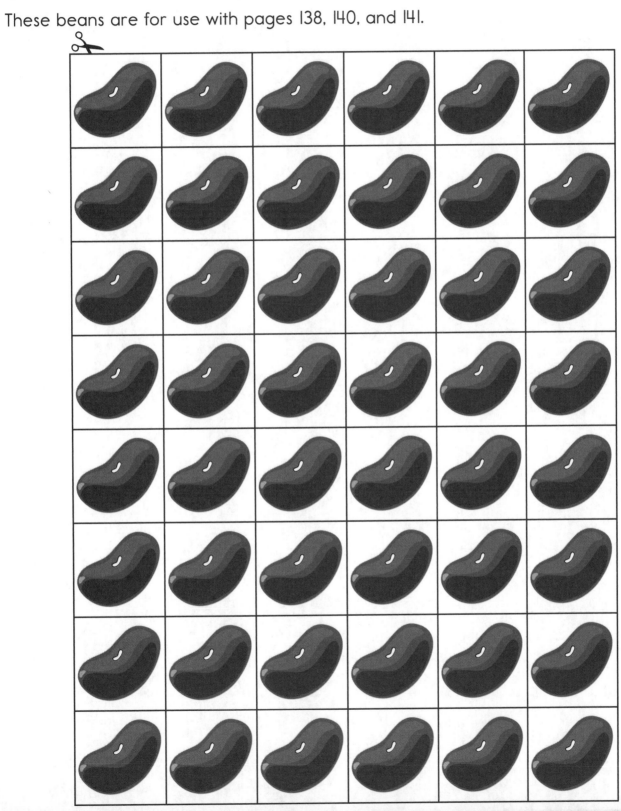

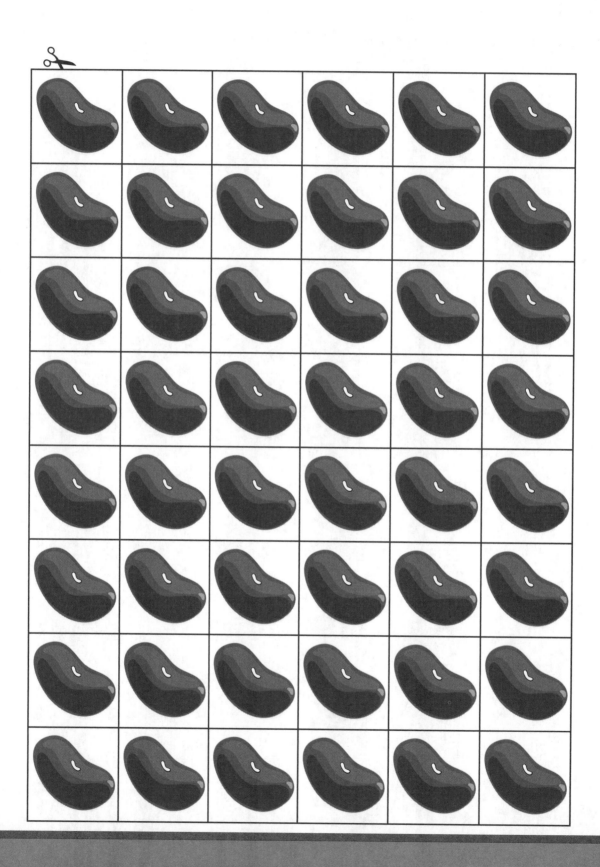

Spinners

CUT OUT the spinner. BEND the outer part of a paper clip so that it points out, and carefully POKE it through the center dot of the spinner. You're ready to spin!

This spinner is for use with page 145, and the reverse side is for use with pages 150 and 151.

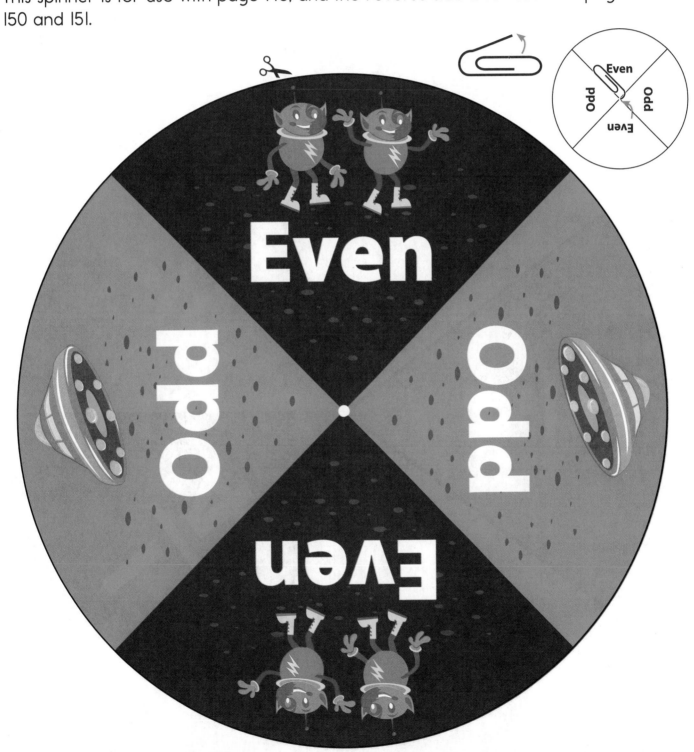

Use the spinner on this side for pages 150 and 151. Pull out the paper clip from the other side, and poke it through the center dot on this side.

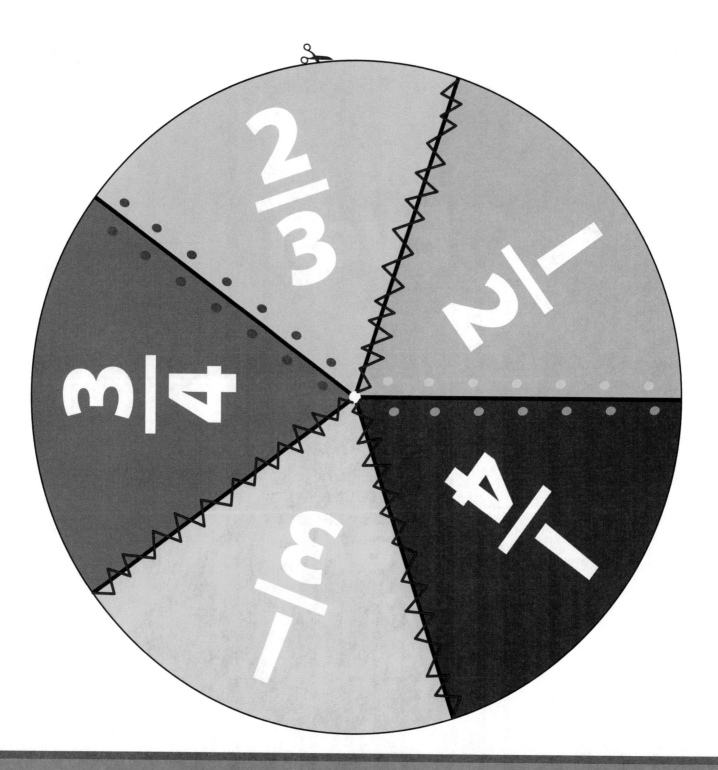

Pattern Blocks

CUT OUT the 31 pattern block pieces.

These pattern block pieces are for use with pages 158, 160, and 161.

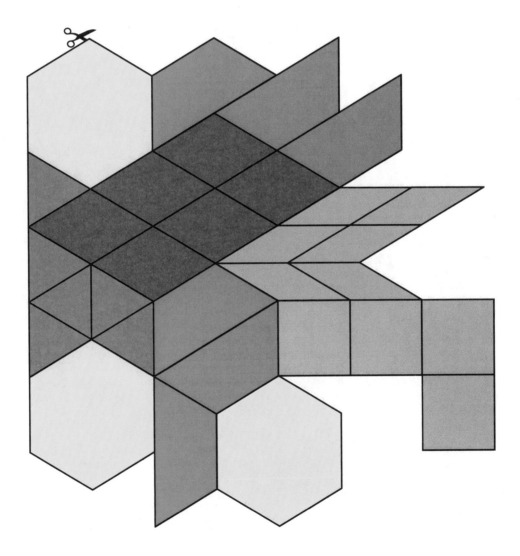

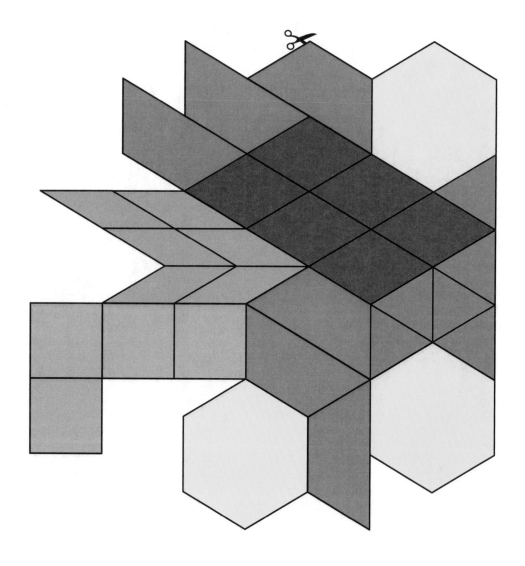

Pentominoes

CUT OUT the 13 pentomino pieces.

These pentomino pieces are for use with pages 162 and 164.

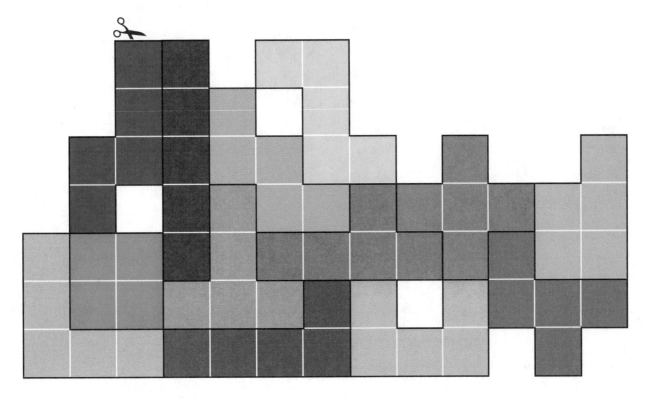

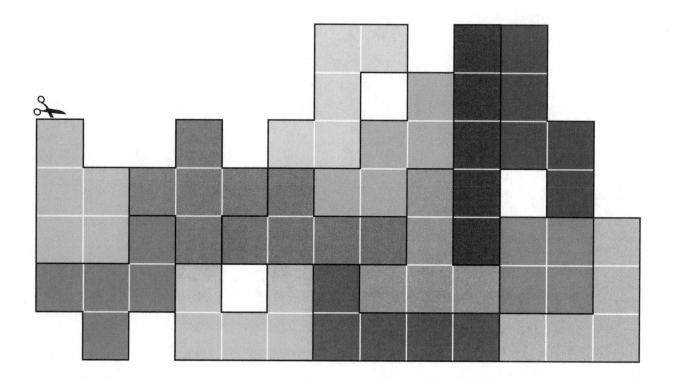

Answers

Page 104

Page 105
1. 364 2. 416 3. 195
4. 608 5. 241
Combination 3 4 1 6 2

Page 106
1. 159 2. 344 3. 506
4. 830 5. 718 6. 472

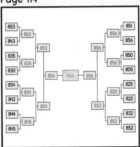

Page 107
Have someone check
your answers.

Page 108
1. 97, 100, 103
2. 215, 218, 220
3. 746, 747, 752, 753
I LIKE YOUR BELT!

Page 109

Page 110

Page 111

10	4	7		175	116	330
20	8	14		168	112	320
30	12	21		161	108	310
40	16	28		154	104	300
50	20	35		147	100	290
60	24	42		140	96	280
70	28	49		133	92	270
80	32	56		126	88	260
90	36	63		119	84	250
100	40	70		112	80	240
110	44	77		105	76	230
120	48	84	91	98	72	220
130	52	56	160	64	68	210
140	150	160	170	180	190	200

Page 112
1. 677 2. 113 3. 742
4. 556 5. 823 6. 256
7. 981 8. 409 9. 187
10. 399

Page 113

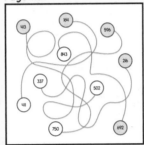

Page 114

853					851
843	853			856	856
835		853			850
830	835		856	850	805
854		854	856		825
842	854			825	822
844		854		852	832
845	845			852	852

Page 115

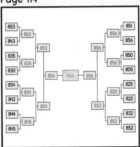

Page 116

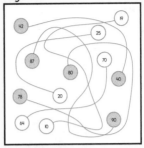

Page 117
Have someone check
your answers.

Page 118
1. 285 2. 544 3. 709
4. 952 5. 549 6. 278
7. 932 8. 717 9. 751

Pages 119–120
Check: 117

Page 121
Check: 81

Page 122
1. 21 2. 16 3. 45
4. 37 5. 62 6. 54

Page 123

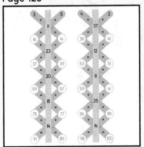

Page 124

3	+	12	=	15
+		+		+
9	+	25	=	34
=		=		=
12	+	37	=	49

Page 125
1. 37 2. 68 3. 59
4. 79 5. 95 6. 48
7. 93 8. 77 9. 63
10. 71 11. 80 12. 91
IT GOES TO PENCILVANIA.

Page 126

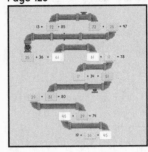

Page 127
Suggestion:

Page 128
1. 12 2. 33 3. 71
4. 48 5. 22 6. 56

Page 129

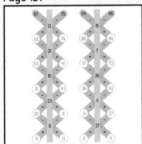

Page 130

95	–	63	=	32
–		–		–
47	–	17	=	30
=		=		=
48	–	46	=	2

Page 131
1. 31 2. 23 3. 2
4. 22 5. 46 6. 49
7. 26 8. 52 9. 13
10. 47 11. 36 12. 16
YOU WOULD HAVE TWO TOYS.

Answers

Page 132

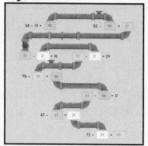

Page 133
Suggestion:

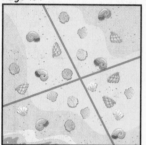

Page 134

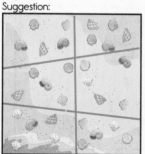

Page 135
1. 3   2. 2   3. 6
4. 2   5. 1   6. 3

Page 136
Suggestion:

Page 137
1. 2   2. 4   3. 2
4. 5   5. 4   6. 2

Page 138
1. 3   2. 5   3. 2
4. 6   5. 8   6. 4

Page 139
Suggestion:

Page 140
1. 4   2. 8   3. 2
4. 7   5. 5   6. 12

Page 142
1. 3   2. 7   3. 9
4. 1   5. 6   6. 12
7. 8   8. 10
TAKE AWAY THE S.

Page 143

Page 144

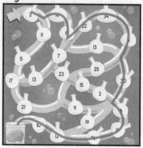

Page 146

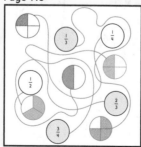

Page 147
Have someone check
your answers.

Page 149

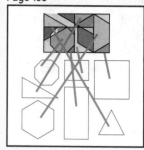

Page 152

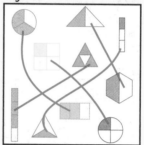

Page 153

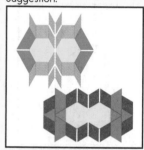

Page 154

1. $\frac{2}{3}$ 2. $\frac{1}{3}$

3. $\frac{4}{4}$ 4. $\frac{1}{2}$

5. $\frac{3}{4}$

Page 155

1. $\frac{1}{3}$ 2. $\frac{3}{4}$

3. $\frac{2}{2}$ 4. $\frac{1}{2}$

5. $\frac{2}{4}$ 6. $\frac{3}{3}$

7. $\frac{2}{3}$ 8. $\frac{4}{4}$

There was a WHOLE IN IT.

Page 156

Page 158
Suggestion:

Page 159

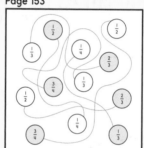

Page 160
Suggestion:

Page 161
Suggestion:

Answers

Page 162
Suggestion:

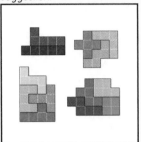

1. 16   2. 18
3. 20   4. 20

Page 163
Have someone check
your answers.

Page 164
Suggestion:

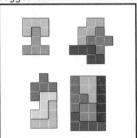

1. 10   2. 15
3. 15   4. 24

Page 165
Have someone check
your answers.

Page 166
1. Monkeys   2. Penguins
3. Polar Bears 4. Elephants
5. Camels   6. Reptiles
7. Lions   8. Sea Lions
9. Zebras   10. Giraffes

Page 167

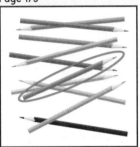

Page 168
1. quarter   2. nickel
3. dime   4. penny

Page 169

Page 170
A FOOTLONG.

Page 171

Page 172
IN SCENTIMETERS.

Page 173

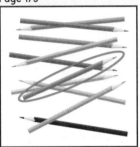

Page 174

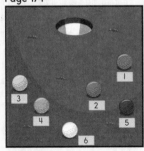

Page 175
Check:
1. 10   2. 12
3. 16   4. 13

Page 176

Page 177
Check:
1. 12   2. 10
3. 7   4. 8
5. 4   6. 13

Page 178
A CLOCK.

Page 179

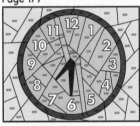

7:30

Page 180
THE LETTER E.

Page 181

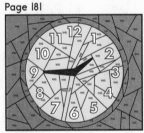

1:45

Page 182

Page 183

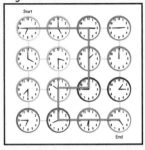

Pages 184–185
1. 1:00   2. 6:45
3. 5:15   4. 12:45
5. 8:00   6. 3:30
7. 2:30   8. 9:30
9. 11:15   10. 5:00
11. 2:15

HE WANTED TO BE ON TIME.

Page 186
1. 30¢   2. 22¢
3. 15¢   4. 51¢
5. 14¢   6. 75¢
7. 25¢   8. 40¢
9. 5¢   10. 41¢
11. 65¢

IT HAS FOUR QUARTERS.

Page 187

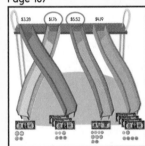

Page 188
1. $1.75   2. $2.02
3. $5.10   4. $6.15
5. $3.50   6. $1.23
7. $2.15   8. $5.60
You HAVE CHANGED.

Page 189

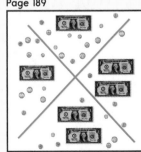

Answers

Page 190
Have someone check
your answers.

Page 193
Extra:

Page 194
1. $1.50   2. $3.07
3. $4.98   4. $6.19
5. $7.45
A COIN.

Page 195
1. 4.98   2. 1.03
3. 6.37   4. 2.29
5. 5.14

Page 196

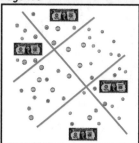

2nd Grade
Math in Action

Take a Seat

Only the first and last seats have the seat numbers marked in each row.
FILL IN the missing numbers.

That Does Not Compute!

The Great Roboto is on the fritz and is spitting out some number sets that have wrong numbers. CIRCLE the wrong numbers in each set.

70   (69)   72   73   74   (57)   76   77

93   94   65   96   97   98   99   10

156   157   158   195   160   161   142   163

203   204   205   201   207   208   202   210

399   401   400   402   403   440   405   406

538   539   530   541   542   543   554   555

Stadium Seating

The seating chart shows the different sections at the baseball stadium. FILL IN the missing numbers.

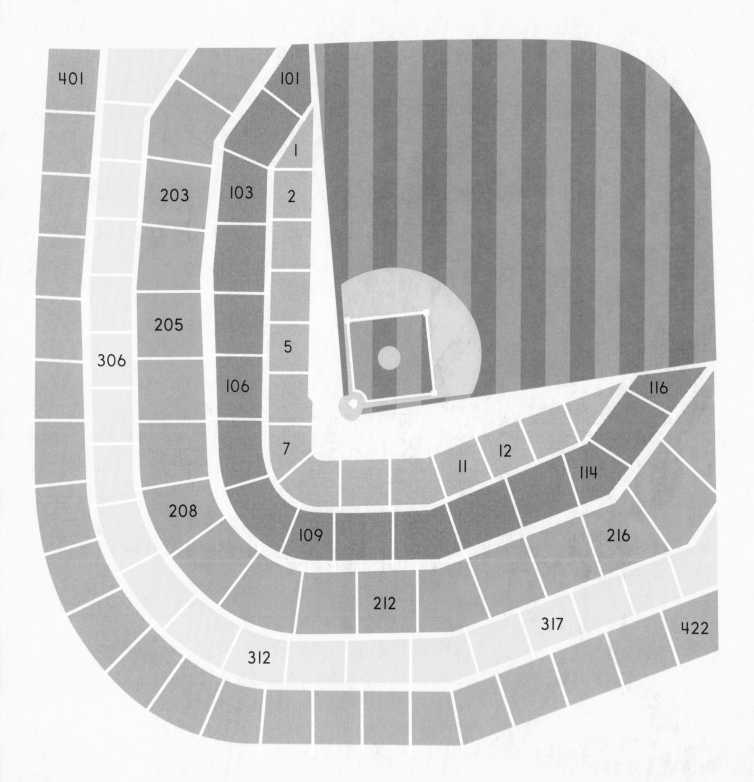

License Plates

Each license plate needs a unique letter and number combination. The license plates are created in numerical order. WRITE the missing numbers on the license plates.

HINT: Write the numbers in order.

Take a Seat

Only the first and last seats have the seat numbers marked in each row. SKIP COUNT by 2, and FILL IN the missing numbers.

Many Marbles

There are nine bags of eight marbles. To find the total number of marbles on this page, SKIP COUNT by 8.

8

1

16

2

3

4

5

6

7

8

9

Going Green

This year, the Martinez family has decided to cut down on their use of electricity by turning off lights and gadgets that aren't being used. They've also switched all of their light bulbs to compact fluorescent light bulbs. They've noticed a decrease in their electricity bills from last year to this year. For each month, CIRCLE the bill that is from this year.

1.

Electric Company
Martinez Family
Billing Month: January
Amount Due: $84

Electric Company
Martinez Family
Billing Month: January
Amount Due: $76

2.

Electric Company
Martinez Family
Billing Month: December
Amount Due: $113

Electric Company
Martinez Family
Billing Month: December
Amount Due: $125

3.

Electric Company
Martinez Family
Billing Month: May
Amount Due: $79

Electric Company
Martinez Family
Billing Month: May
Amount Due: $91

4.

Electric Company
Martinez Family
Billing Month: August
Amount Due: $158

Electric Company
Martinez Family
Billing Month: August
Amount Due: $132

High Score

The high scores on the left are sorted by name. WRITE a new high score list starting with the highest score and ending with the lowest score.

HIGH SCORES	
AMY	568
DAN	421
JIN	799
KEN	645
MAX	736
MIA	806
SAM	279
TED	310

HIGH SCORES		
1.		
2.		
3.		
4.		
5.		
6.		
7.		
8.		

Super Skyscrapers

CIRCLE the name of the taller building in each pair.

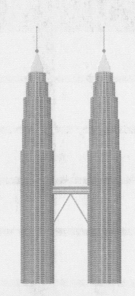

Willis Tower
Chicago
442 meters

Petronas Towers
Kuala Lumpur
452 meters

U.S. Bank Tower
Los Angeles
310 meters

Empire State Building
New York
381 meters

Jin Mao Tower
Shanghai
420 meters

1. Empire State Building   Willis Tower

2. Petronas Towers   U.S. Bank Tower

3. Willis Tower   Petronas Towers

4. Jin Mao Tower   U.S. Bank Tower

5. Willis Tower   Jin Mao Tower

6. U.S. Bank Tower   Empire State Building

7. Petronas Towers   Jin Mao Tower

8. Jin Mao Tower   Empire State Building

Ask the Judges

The gymnasts' scores have been tallied, and each gymnast is holding her score. WRITE the numbers 1 through 6 above each gymnast so that 1 is the gymnast with the highest score, and 6 is the gymnast with the lowest score.

Scout Sales

The scouts in the Scrantonville Scout Troop are selling wrapping paper to raise money for their upcoming camping trip. They want to get a rough count of how much has been sold so far. ROUND the number of rolls of wrapping paper sold by each scout to the nearest ten.

HINT: Numbers that end in 1 through 4 get rounded down to the nearest ten, and numbers that end in 5 through 9 get rounded up to the nearest ten.

1. Victoria   28 rolls   __30__ rolls

2. Julia   42 rolls   _____ rolls

3. Emily   59 rolls   _____ rolls

4. Jessica   13 rolls   _____ rolls

5. Taylor   96 rolls   _____ rolls

6. Jacqueline   81 rolls   _____ rolls

7. Makayla   77 rolls   _____ rolls

8. Briana   65 rolls   _____ rolls

9. Jada   24 rolls   _____ rolls

10. Sierra   86 rolls   _____ rolls

11. Claire   35 rolls   _____ rolls

12. Andrea   54 rolls   _____ rolls

Driving Distances

Rounding distances makes it easier to calculate travel times. ROUND the miles between each pair of cities to the nearest hundred.

HINT: Numbers that end in 1 through 49 get rounded down to the nearest hundred, and numbers that end in 50 through 99 get rounded up to the nearest hundred.

1. Chicago to Kansas City   532 miles   <u>500</u> miles

2. New Orleans to Memphis   396 miles   _____ miles

3. Detroit to Indianapolis   318 miles   _____ miles

4. Toronto to St. Louis   782 miles   _____ miles

5. Boston to New York   215 miles   _____ miles

6. Las Vegas to Albuquerque   578 miles   _____ miles

7. Los Angeles to San Francisco   385 miles   _____ miles

8. Dallas to Omaha   669 miles   _____ miles

9. Houston to El Paso   758 miles   _____ miles

10. Seattle to Vancouver   140 miles   _____ miles

Flower Garden

Iris just moved into a house with a beautiful flower garden. She wants to plant the same number of flowers next year, but she doesn't know how many plants to buy. ESTIMATE the number of flowers in the garden. Then COUNT to check your estimate.

Estimate: _____   Check: _____

Toy Tower

A toy store is giving away a prize to anyone who can guess the number of blocks in the tower. ESTIMATE the number of blocks. Then COUNT to check your estimate.

Estimate: 　　　　　Check:

Adding & Subtracting

Pay the Check

WRITE the total on each restaurant check.

1.

GUEST CHECK

Date	Table	Guests	Server	100036

Spaghetti with meatballs	$14
Chicken salad	$11
Total	$

2.

GUEST CHECK

Date	Table	Guests	Server	100037

Burritos	$22
Chicken tacos	$16
Total	$

3.

GUEST CHECK

Date	Table	Guests	Server	100038

Grilled steak	$35
Lobster chowder	$11
Mushroom ravioli	$23
Total	$

4.

GUEST CHECK

Date	Table	Guests	Server	100039

Grilled salmon	$41
Beef short ribs	$26
Chocolate cake	$10
Total	$

Ask the Judges

The winner of the dance competition is the one with the highest score out of 100 possible points. ADD each dancer's scores. Then CIRCLE the winning dancer.

| 42 | 48 | 43 | 36 | 50 | 32 |
| 37 | 40 | 54 | 43 | 44 | 27 |

Adding & Subtracting

High Score

These four kids are all trying to get the high score. ADD their scores, and CIRCLE the person with the highest score.

1.

Player 1	
	3 2
	2 1
	1 5
Total Score	

2.

Player 2	
	1 6
	5 2
	1 0
Total Score	

3.

Player 3	
	3 5
	3 4
	1 0
Total Score	

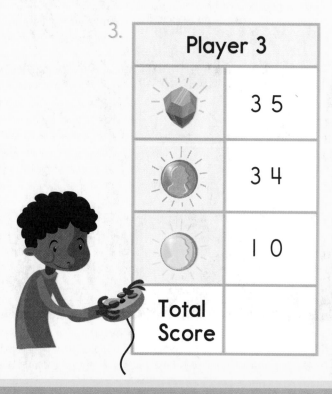

4.

Player 4	
	2 6
	2 1
	1 1
Total Score	

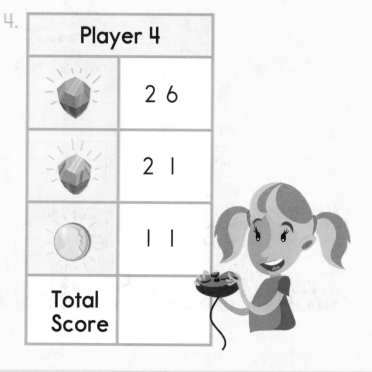

Piggy Bank

Each piggy bank shows how much money a kid has saved. If each kid takes $22 out of the bank to spend on a new DVD, WRITE the new amount in each piggy bank.

 $56 $ ____
1

 $92 $ ____
2

 $38 $ ____
3

 $45 $ ____
4

 $67 $ ____
5

 $24 $ ____
6

Zoo Crew

Today the zoologists are studying the lengths of the different reptiles at the zoo. The new Komodo dragon is 98 inches long. WRITE the difference in length between the Komodo dragon and the other reptiles.

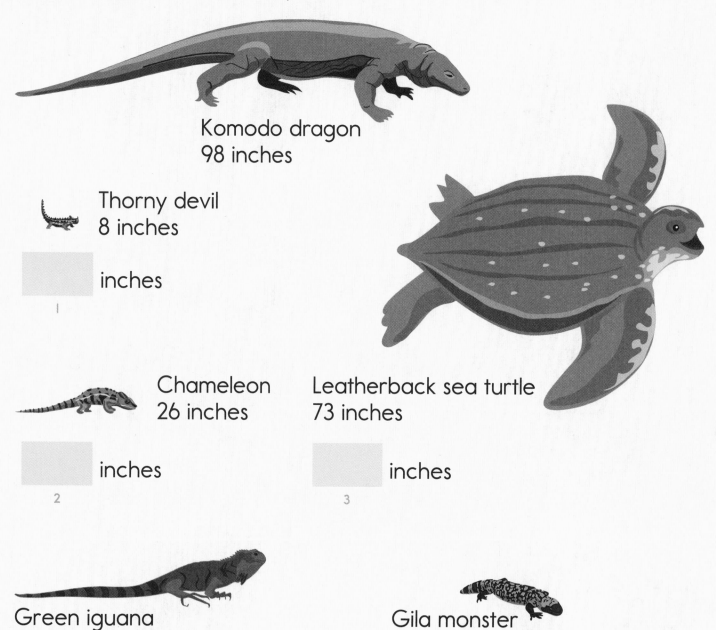

Komodo dragon
98 inches

Thorny devil
8 inches

_____ inches

1

Chameleon
26 inches

_____ inches

2

Leatherback sea turtle
73 inches

_____ inches

3

Green iguana
54 inches

_____ inches

4

Gila monster
22 inches

_____ inches

5

Best Price

Ann is shopping for the best price on a video game player. Each store has it for a different price, and Ann was able to find a coupon for each store. CIRCLE the video game player with the best price if Ann uses the coupon.

$75

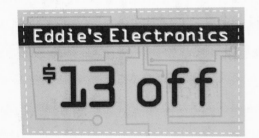

Eddie's Electronics
$13 off

$88

SUPERSTAR SUPERCADE
$15 OFF

$72

Buy It Now!
$12 OFF

$84

Gotcha Game
$10 OFF

Adding with Regrouping

Amusement Adventures

Each ride is shown with the number of riders it had on Friday morning and Friday afternoon. WRITE the total number of riders for each ride on Friday.

1.

Morning	Afternoon	Total
36	45	81

2.

Morning	Afternoon	Total
24	29	

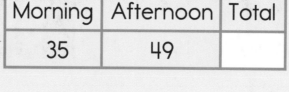

3.

Morning	Afternoon	Total
35	49	

4.

Morning	Afternoon	Total
36	37	

5.

Morning	Afternoon	Total
19	25	

6.

Morning	Afternoon	Total
42	48	

7.

Morning	Afternoon	Total
39	39	

Comfort Couch Car

READ the paragraph, and WRITE the answer.

Beckett loves inventing things, and one day he built his best invention yet, the Comfort Couch Car. After Beckett zoomed out of the driveway, he sped 16 blocks to Main Street. Then he turned left and went another 25 blocks. On Pine Street, he took a right and went 12 blocks before he had to stop at a stoplight. Then he went 18 blocks more to get to his friend Shawn's house to show off his Comfort Couch Car. How many blocks did Beckett travel?

blocks

High Score

Someone just beat the high score of 132 points in Galaxy Treasure Trove! Was it Ben or Akimi? ADD their scores, and CIRCLE the person who has the new high score.

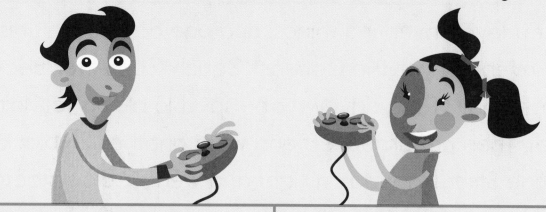

Ben		Akimi	
	27		45
	42		40
	15		23
	21		18
	6		12
1. Total Score		2. Total Score	

Pay the Check

WRITE the total on each restaurant check.

1.

GUEST CHECK	
Date Table Guests Server	100040
BBQ pork	$18
Cheeseburger deluxe	$15
Total	$

2.

GUEST CHECK	
Date Table Guests Server	100041
Sea scallops	$25
Fish and chips	$19
Total	$

3.

GUEST CHECK	
Date Table Guests Server	100042
Penne in tomato sauce	$23
Lasagna	$27
Cheese ravioli	$18
Total	$

4.

GUEST CHECK	
Date Table Guests Server	100043
Roasted sea bass	$35
Rack of lamb	$29
Roast chicken	$16
Total	$

Subtracting with Regrouping

City Blocks

WRITE the number of blocks each person has to travel.

HINT: Subtract the smaller street number from the larger street number.

1. Joey is on 82nd Street, and he needs to go to 37th Street. _____ blocks

2. Amanda is leaving 14th Street to go to 42nd Street. _____ blocks

3. Izzy is on 23rd Street and is on her way up to 71st Street. _____ blocks

4. Satchel needs to go to 33rd Street from 4th Street. _____ blocks

5. Brianna is headed to 55th Street. Right now she is at 92nd Street. _____ blocks

6. Luis is on 31st Street, and he needs to go to 50th Street. _____ blocks

7. Hunter is leaving 84th Street to go to 19th Street. _____ blocks

8. Alexis is on 66th street and is on her way down to 28th Street. _____ blocks

Zoo Crew

Today the zoologists are studying the weights of the different primates at the zoo. The heaviest primate at the zoo is the chimpanzee, weighing 91 pounds. WRITE the difference in weight between the chimpanzee and the other primates.

**Chimpanzee
91 pounds**

**Ring-tailed lemur
5 pounds**

_____ **pounds**

1

**Mandrill
72 pounds**

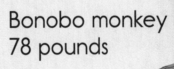

**Bonobo monkey
78 pounds**

_____ **pounds**

2

_____ **pounds**

3

**Olive baboon
64 pounds**

**Hoolock gibbon
15 pounds**

_____ **pounds**

4

_____ **pounds**

5

235

Best Price

Jorge is shopping for the best price on a tennis racket. Each store has one for a different price, and Jorge was able to find a coupon for each store. CIRCLE the tennis racket with the best price if Jorge uses the coupon.

$52

Sporty Store

$15 OFF

$61

ANN'S
ATHLETIC SUPPLY
$25 OFF

$55

SPORT PORT

$16 off

$67

TENNISVILLE

$18 off

That Does Not Compute!

The Great Roboto is on the fritz and is spitting out some math problems with wrong answers. CIRCLE the incorrect differences.

64 – 15 = 49

34 – 29 = 6

41 – 27 = 16

93 – 58 = 35

82 – 34 = 46

56 – 19 = 37

66 – 58 = 8

75 – 46 = 39

95 – 18 = 77

33 – 9 = 25

45 – 17 = 28

81 – 23 = 68

Grouping

Kate's Kitchen

Today in Kate's Kitchen, Kate is making gift bags of muffins. Each bag holds five muffins. WRITE the number of bags Kate will use to package all of the muffins.

bags

Camp Counselors

Murray, the head counselor of Camp Cowabunga, is dividing the campers into groups. There are 3 counselors and 24 campers. WRITE the number of campers that will be with each counselor.

Mason Carlos Kaylee

Erin Tim Amber

Trevor Marcus

Cheyenne Cody Alex

Adam Katelyn

Devin Miguel Allison Katie

Sophia

Seth Jeremy

Olivia

Adelaine Ian Isaiah

campers per counselor

Hot Dog Dilemma

Hot dogs come 10 to a package, but hot dog buns come 8 to a package. CIRCLE the smallest number of packages of hot dogs and hot dog buns you could buy so that you end up with the same number of hot dogs and hot dog buns.

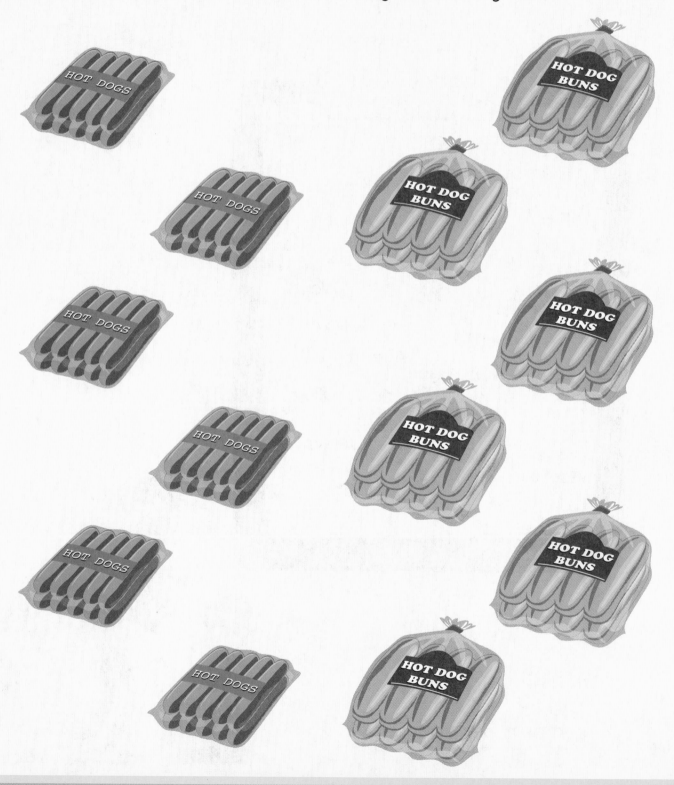

Save the Day

Armie the Armazing has spotted a sinking ship with 24 people onboard. He can carry a total of 4 people. WRITE the number of trips Armie must make to the boat to rescue all of the people.

trips

Earthly Gadgets

Two aliens have gathered 16 interesting earth gadgets and want to take them home to their different planets. If they split the gadgets equally, WRITE the number of gadgets each alien will take home.

gadgets

Fries with Friends

Three friends are always trying to take more than their fair share. They're about to share 18 french fries. Help the friends share them equally. WRITE the number of french fries each friend should get.

french fries

Wiener Dogs

Danny's three dachshunds love delicious sausages. Danny wants to give each dog four slices of sausage. WRITE the number of sausage slices Danny should cut for his dogs.

slices

Once Upon a Time

Snow White has been picking berries in the forest for the seven dwarves. She picked 35 berries. WRITE the number of berries each dwarf will get if the dwarves share the berries equally.

_____ berries

Save the Day

Superhero Even Steven is hot on the trail of a criminal known only as The Oddball. The Oddball leaves his signature at every crime: an odd number of bouncy balls. The trouble is there are now copycat crimes all over town. Help Even Steven and CIRCLE the crime scenes of The Oddball.

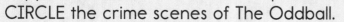

Once Upon a Time

Hansel and Gretel have tricked the evil witch and are leaving her sugarcoated house, but before they go, they decide to take some sweets with them. They want to take candy that comes in even numbers so they can share it equally on the way home. CIRCLE the kinds of candy Hansel and Gretel will take with them.

Not the Whole Cookie

If you are too full to eat a whole cookie, Bob's Bakery will make you a cookie any size you want. CIRCLE the cookie that matches each person's order.

I'd like $\frac{1}{2}$ of a cookie, please.

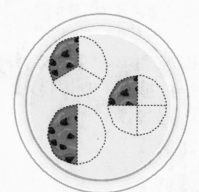

Please give me $\frac{3}{4}$ of a cookie.

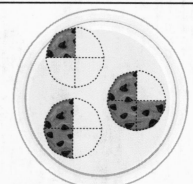

I'll take $\frac{2}{3}$ of a cookie, please.

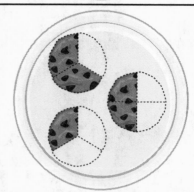

Just $\frac{1}{4}$ of a cookie for me, please.

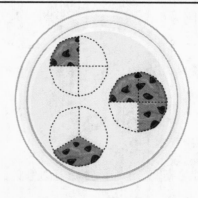

Kate's Kitchen

Today in Kate's Kitchen, Kate is making chocolate-covered bananas. CIRCLE the right amount of each ingredient needed for the recipe.

Chocolate-Covered Bananas

$\frac{1}{4}$ stick of butter

$\frac{2}{3}$ bar of dark chocolate

$\frac{1}{2}$ banana

Melt the butter and chocolate in a small saucepan. Put the banana on a wooden stick and dip it into the melted chocolate mixture until it's covered. Let it cool on a piece of wax paper.

Recognizing Fractions

Flower Box

Sheila planted a flower box for her windowsill. It had $\frac{1}{2}$ orange daisies, $\frac{1}{4}$ white daisies, and $\frac{1}{4}$ yellow daisies. CIRCLE the flower box that Sheila planted.

Flag Designer

COLOR each flag according to the fractions.

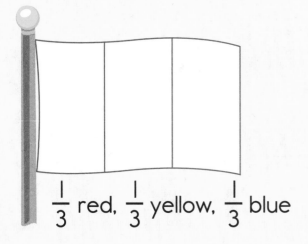

$\frac{1}{3}$ red, $\frac{1}{3}$ yellow, $\frac{1}{3}$ blue

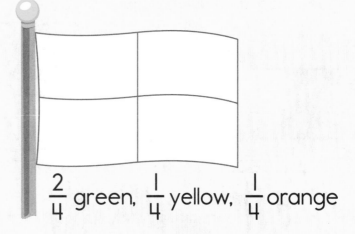

$\frac{2}{4}$ green, $\frac{1}{4}$ yellow, $\frac{1}{4}$ orange

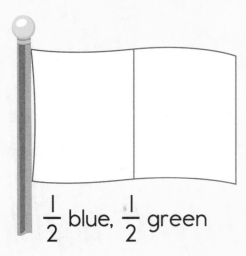

$\frac{1}{2}$ blue, $\frac{1}{2}$ green

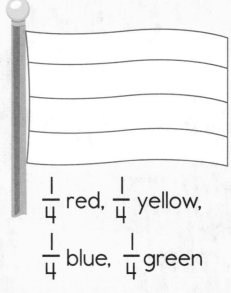

$\frac{1}{4}$ red, $\frac{1}{4}$ yellow, $\frac{1}{4}$ blue, $\frac{1}{4}$ green

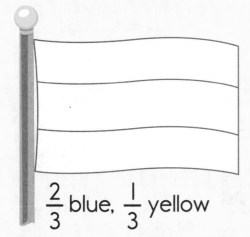

$\frac{2}{3}$ blue, $\frac{1}{3}$ yellow

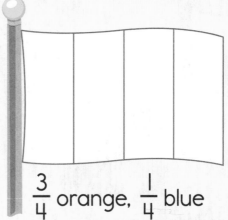

$\frac{3}{4}$ orange, $\frac{1}{4}$ blue

That Does Not Compute!

The Great Roboto is on the fritz and is spitting out some wrong fractions. He was programmed to print pictures showing $\frac{3}{4}$. CIRCLE the pictures that do **not** show $\frac{3}{4}$ of the shape colored.

Sandwich Snackers

WRITE the fraction of sandwich each person has left.

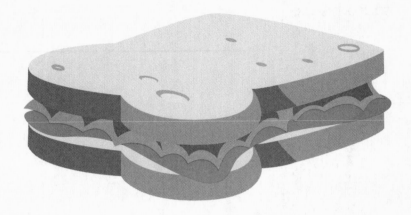

1. Elsie had a sandwich cut into two equal pieces.
   She ate one of the pieces.

   ———

2. Roger had a sandwich cut into four equal pieces.
   He ate two of the pieces and gave one piece to Jane.

   ———

3. Brent had a sandwich cut into three equal pieces.
   He ate one of the pieces.

   ———

4. Evelina had a sandwich cut into four equal pieces.
   She ate one of the pieces.

   ———

5. Joshua had a sandwich cut into three equal pieces.
   He ate one of the pieces and gave one of the pieces
   to Rachel.

   ———

Share the Pie

Garrett got $\frac{3}{4}$ of a pie, a piece much too big for him to eat. He wants to share his pie with the person who got the smallest fraction of pie. CIRCLE the person with whom Garrett should share his pie.

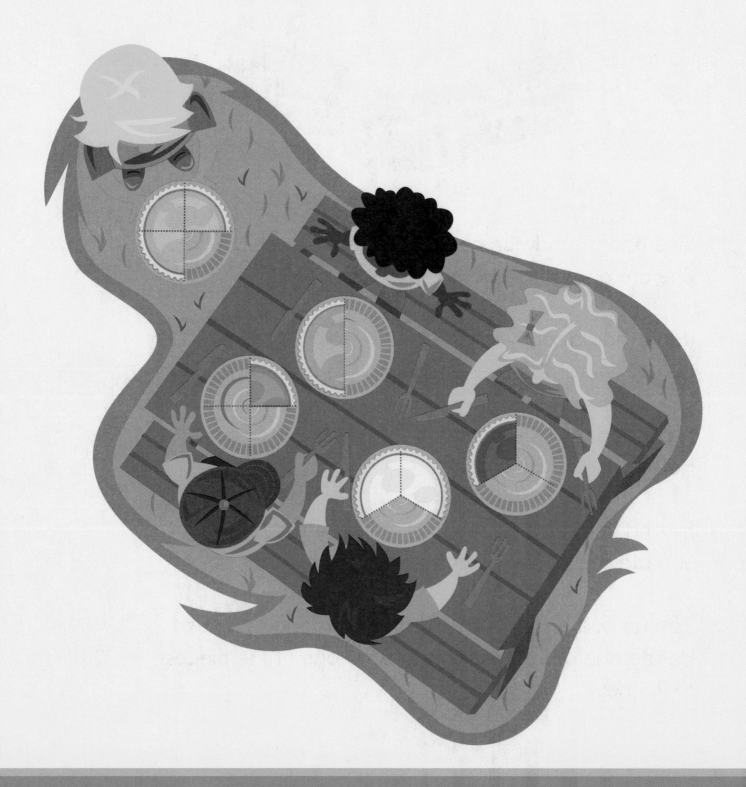

Going Green

One neighborhood is going green by recycling and reusing to reduce the amount of trash thrown away. Pairs of neighbors have challenged each other to throw away the least amount of trash. WRITE the fraction of trash that you see in each trash can. Then, for each pair of trash cans, CIRCLE the trash can of the neighbor with the least amount of trash.

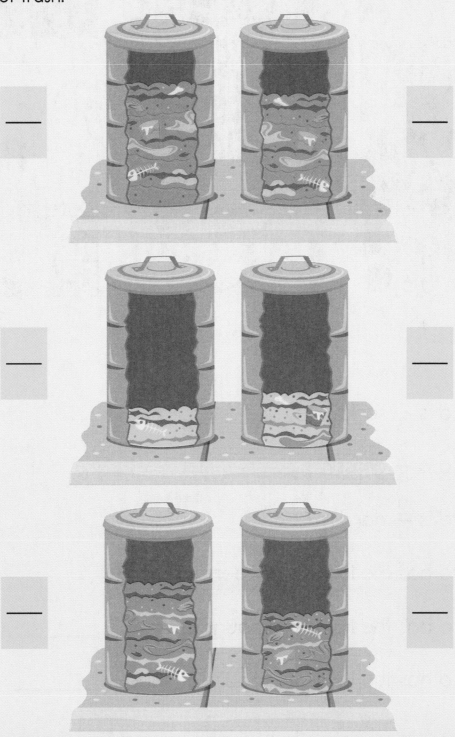

Yard Use

WRITE the number of the yard that matches each description.

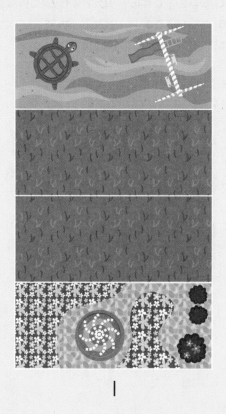
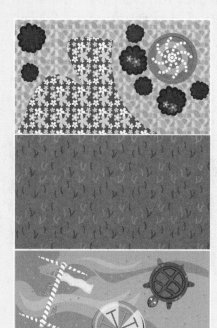

1   2   3

1. Which yard is $\frac{1}{3}$ sand? _____

2. Which yard is $\frac{2}{4}$ grass? _____

3. Which yard is $\frac{2}{4}$ garden? _____

4. Which yard has the largest garden? _____

5. Which yard has the largest amount of grass? _____

6. Which yard has the largest amount of sand? _____

Frisbee Fling

COLOR each Frisbee according to the fractions. Then CIRCLE the Frisbee in each pair that has the larger fraction of blue.

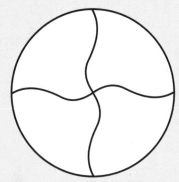

$\frac{2}{4}$ blue, $\frac{1}{4}$ red, $\frac{1}{4}$ green

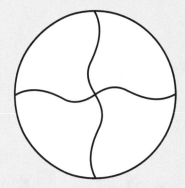

$\frac{1}{4}$ yellow, $\frac{3}{4}$ blue

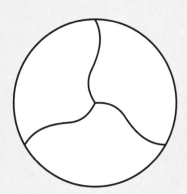

$\frac{1}{3}$ orange, $\frac{1}{3}$ blue, $\frac{1}{3}$ green

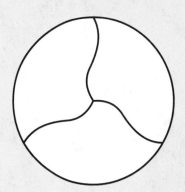

$\frac{2}{3}$ blue, $\frac{1}{3}$ red

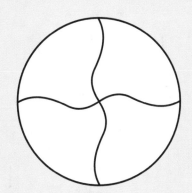

$\frac{1}{4}$ orange, $\frac{2}{4}$ blue, $\frac{1}{4}$ yellow

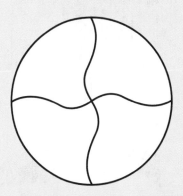

$\frac{1}{4}$ blue, $\frac{1}{4}$ red, $\frac{1}{4}$ yellow, $\frac{1}{4}$ orange

That Does Not Compute!

The Great Roboto is on the fritz and is spitting out some incorrect inequalities. CIRCLE each wrong inequality.

$$\frac{1}{4} > \frac{1}{2}$$

$$\frac{3}{4} > \frac{2}{3}$$

$$\frac{1}{2} < \frac{3}{4}$$

$$\frac{3}{4} < \frac{1}{3}$$

$$\frac{1}{4} < \frac{2}{4}$$

$$\frac{1}{3} > \frac{2}{3}$$

$$\frac{1}{4} = \frac{1}{3}$$

$$\frac{2}{4} = \frac{1}{2}$$

Kate's Kitchen

Today in Kate's Kitchen, Kate is making four different recipes for smoothies.
WRITE the number of the recipe that has the largest amount of each ingredient.

Smoothie 1

$\frac{2}{3}$ banana

$\frac{3}{4}$ cup plain yogurt

$\frac{1}{2}$ cup apple juice

$\frac{1}{4}$ mango

Smoothie 2

$\frac{1}{4}$ banana

$\frac{1}{4}$ cup plain yogurt

$\frac{3}{4}$ cup apple juice

$\frac{1}{3}$ mango

Smoothie 3

$\frac{1}{2}$ banana

$\frac{2}{3}$ cup plain yogurt

$\frac{1}{3}$ cup apple juice

$\frac{1}{2}$ mango

Smoothie 4

$\frac{1}{4}$ banana

$\frac{1}{2}$ cup plain yogurt

$\frac{1}{4}$ cup apple juice

$\frac{2}{3}$ mango

banana _____

plain yogurt _____

apple juice _____

mango _____

Block Bin

Jake's mom wants to find a bin to store all of his building blocks, but she needs to make sure that it fits on the shelf. She measured the shelf using the building blocks, and the space is 12 building blocks long. CIRCLE the largest bin she could buy to fit the space.

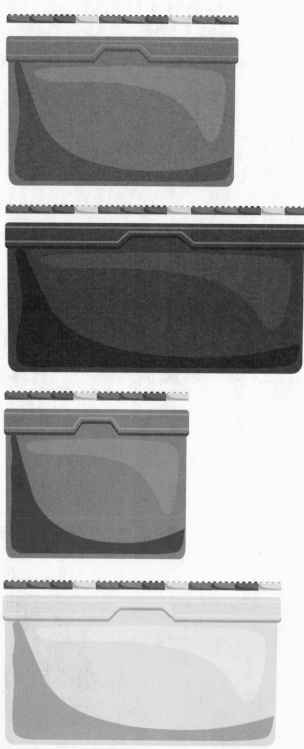

Zoo Crew

Today the zoologists are measuring the small aquarium animals at the zoo. They can be difficult to measure, so the zoologists are using the rocks at the bottom of the tank to measure the length of each animal. WRITE the length of each animal in rocks.

Water turtle

_____ rocks
1

Catfish

_____ rocks
2

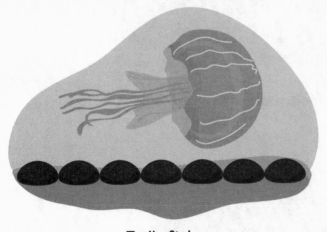

Jellyfish

_____ rocks
3

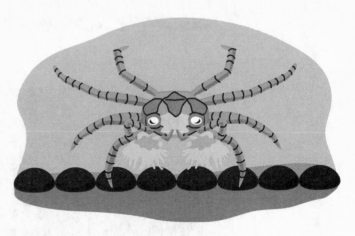

Boxer crab

_____ rocks
4

Sofa Squeeze

Sonya is going shopping for a new sofa, and she wants to make sure it will fit. She measures the space by using her feet. The space is equal to 10 of her feet, heel to toe. CIRCLE the largest sofa that will fit in Sonya's space.

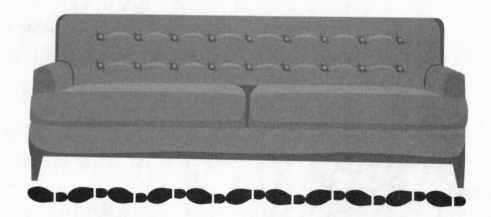

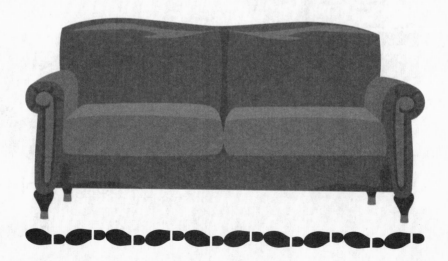

Field Trip

TAKE 10 pennies into your kitchen and PUT them in a row. FIND things that measure about 10 pennies, less than 10 pennies, and more than 10 pennies. WRITE what you find.

About 10 Pennies

Less than 10 Pennies

More than 10 Pennies

Zoo Crew

Today the zoologists are identifying insects based on their length. The list shows the name of each insect and its length in inches (in.). WRITE the correct name next to each insect.

Hissing cockroach: 3 in.   Leaf insect: 4 in.

Katydid: 2 in.   Praying mantis: 5 in.

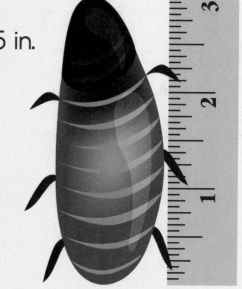

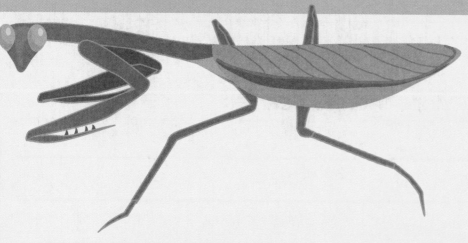

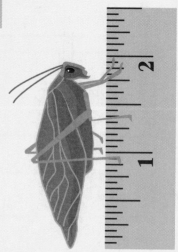

Save the Day

Sammy the Supersmall Superhero is in trouble! The diabolical Clancy the Clone has made copies of Sammy, and no one knows who the real Sammy is. The only clue is that Sammy is 3 inches tall. CIRCLE the real Sammy the Supersmall Superhero.

Field Trip

TAKE an inch ruler with you to the grocery store. FIND things that measure about 6 inches, less than 6 inches, and more than 6 inches. WRITE what you find.

About 6 Inches

_____

_____

_____

_____

Less than 6 Inches

_____

_____

_____

_____

More than 6 Inches

_____

_____

_____

_____

Nailed It

Tina is hanging a picture and needs just the right nail for the job. If it's too short, it won't hold the picture. If it's too long, it will go through the wall. She needs a nail that's 5 centimeters long. CIRCLE the nail Tina should use.

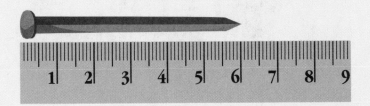

Rainy Days

A rain gauge measures how much rain has fallen. WRITE the number of centimeters (cm) of rain that has fallen at each location.

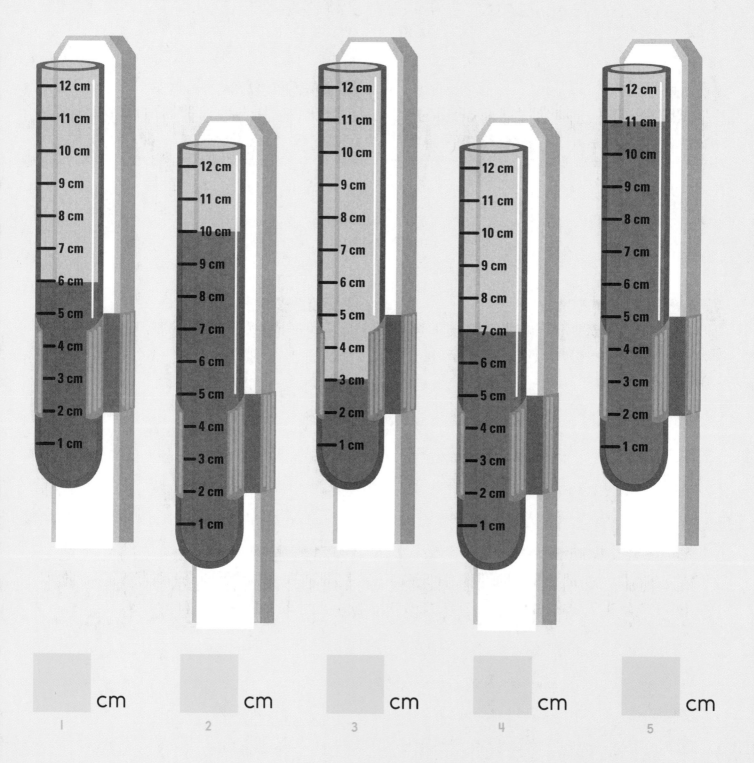

cm	cm	cm	cm	cm
1	2	3	4	5

Lost Lizard

Justin brought his lizard over to his friend Jocelyn's house. She has three lizards. It's time to go, and now Justin is having a hard time telling which lizard is his. He knows it's 11 centimeters long. CIRCLE Justin's lizard.

Which Window?

Tracey is putting the finishing touches on her tree house, and she wants to add a window. The plans call for a rectangular window that has a perimeter of 36 inches. CIRCLE the window Tracey should get.

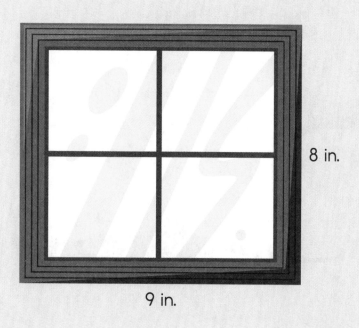

8 in.

9 in.

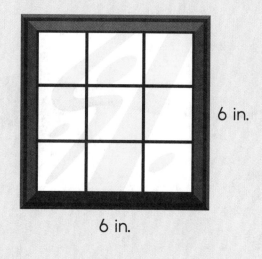

6 in.

6 in.

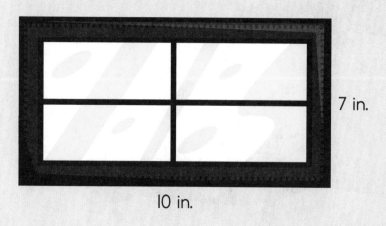

7 in.

10 in.

10 in.

8 in.

Kite Competition

Four children have entered their kites in a kite competition for the largest kite. The kite with the largest perimeter wins. WRITE the perimeter of each kite. Then CIRCLE the winning kite.

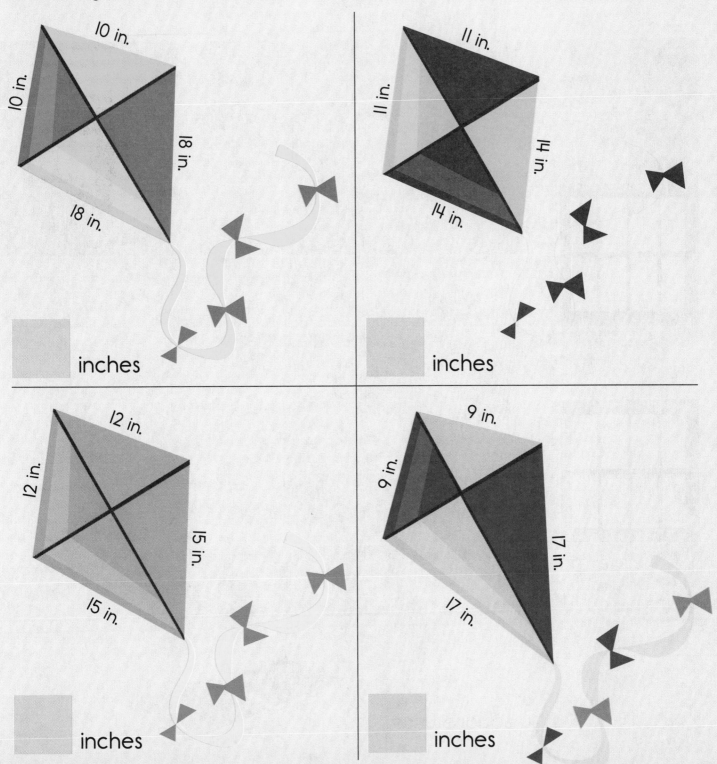

Going Green

The Tarrytown Town Hall city manager wants to install a "green" roof on the town hall to save on heating and cooling costs. The roof comes in square blocks. WRITE the area of usable roof space so the city manager knows how many roof blocks to order.

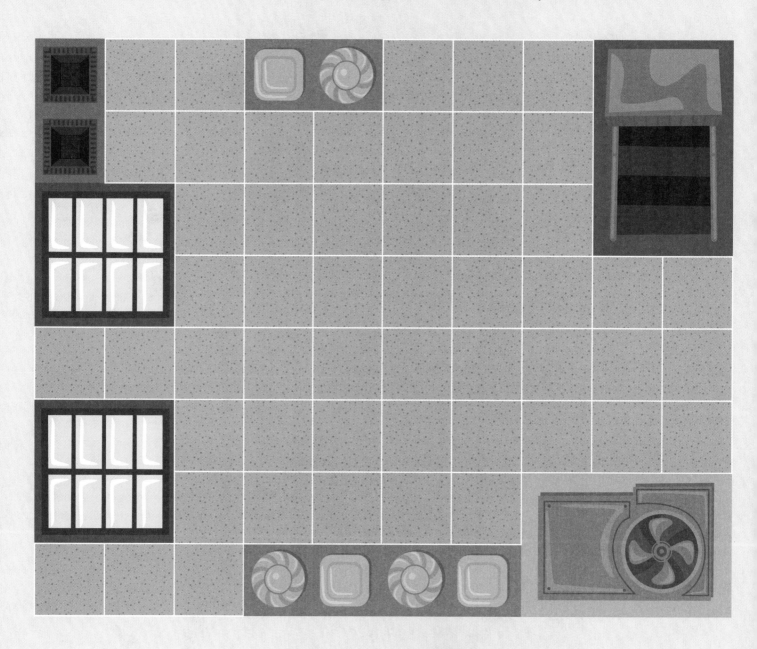

square units

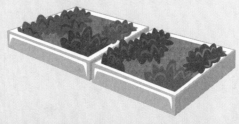

Paint Job

The area of this wall is 40 square units. COLOR the wall so that 15 square units are green, 12 square units are orange, and 13 square units are yellow.

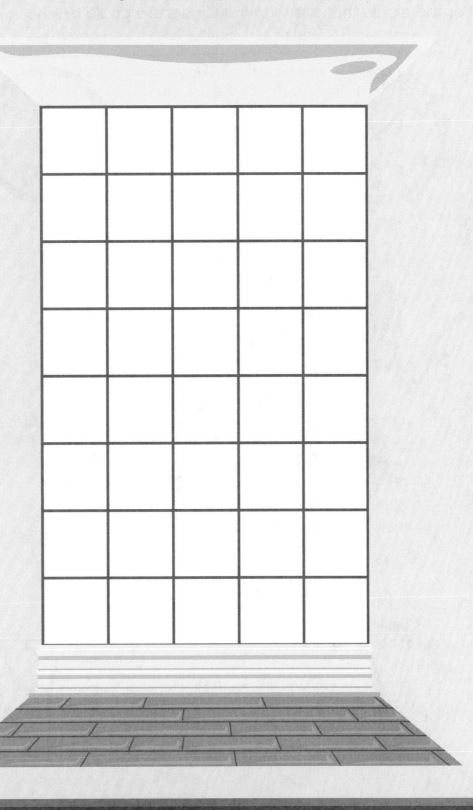

Once Upon a Time

It's the night of the ball, and Cinderella wants to get some shopping done before her carriage turns into a pumpkin at midnight. If each clock shown is at night, CIRCLE all of the clocks that show a time Cinderella could be shopping.

Time Pieces

Can you help fix the broken clocks? CIRCLE the clock hand that is missing from each clock.

1. **2:00**

2. **4:30**

3. **7:00**

4. **11:30**

Save the Day

The Mighty Minuto got a note that said the evil villain The Time Turner is going to be in the clock tower that is set to 4:15. CIRCLE the clock tower where The Mighty Minuto can catch The Time Turner.

Time Pieces

Can you help fix the broken clocks? CIRCLE the clock hand that is missing from each clock.

Time Zones

Most of North America is divided into four main time zones: Eastern Time, Central Time, Mountain Time, and Pacific Time. There is a one-hour difference between each time zone. Each clock shows a time in one of the time zones. WRITE the time it would be in another time zone.

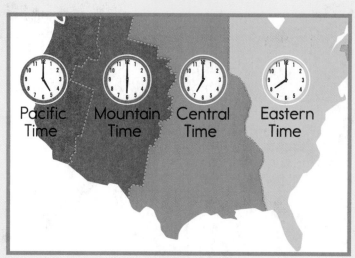

Pacific Time   Mountain Time   Central Time   Eastern Time

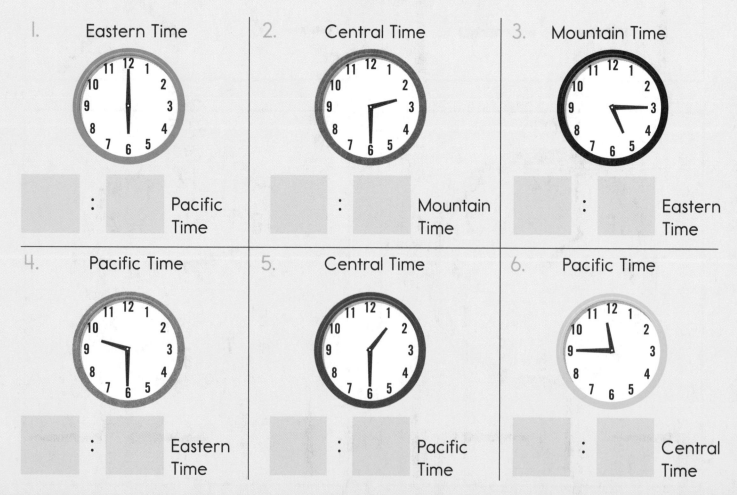

1. Eastern Time

☐ ☐ : ☐ ☐ Pacific Time

2. Central Time

☐ ☐ : ☐ ☐ Mountain Time

3. Mountain Time

☐ ☐ : ☐ ☐ Eastern Time

4. Pacific Time

☐ ☐ : ☐ ☐ Eastern Time

5. Central Time

☐ ☐ : ☐ ☐ Pacific Time

6. Pacific Time

☐ ☐ : ☐ ☐ Central Time

Round Trip

The Garcia family has a busy schedule. WRITE the amount of time (which includes travel time) that the family needs for each activity.

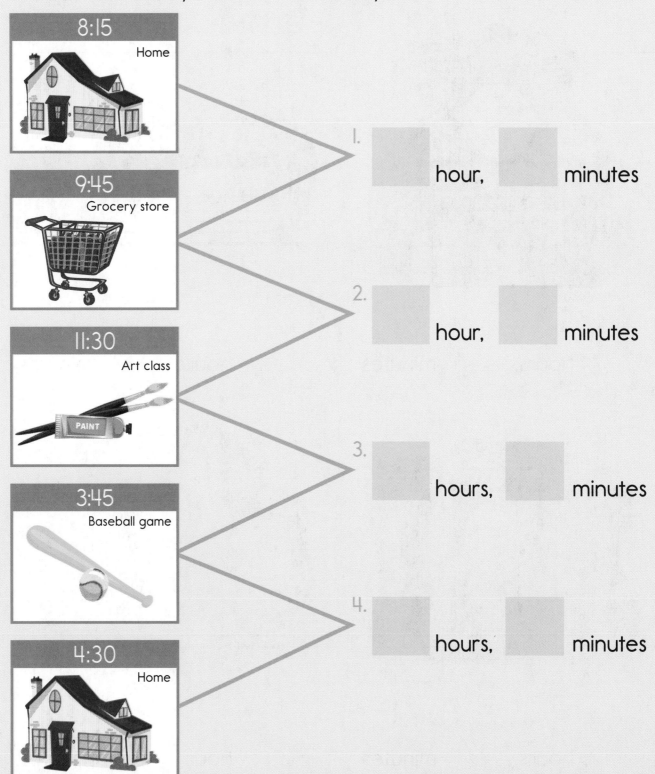

8:15 Home

9:45 Grocery store

11:30 Art class

3:45 Baseball game

4:30 Home

1. ☐ hour, ☐ minutes

2. ☐ hour, ☐ minutes

3. ☐ hours, ☐ minutes

4. ☐ hours, ☐ minutes

Time on the Train

The train gets into the final station at 9:00. WRITE how much time is left on the train ride at each station.

1. ☐ hours, ☐ minutes

2. ☐ hours, ☐ minutes

3. ☐ hours, ☐ minutes

4. ☐ hour, ☐ minutes

Party Time

The first clock shows the time the party started, and the second clock shows the time the party ended. WRITE how long each party lasted.

1. ☐ hours, ☐ minutes

2. ☐ hours, ☐ minutes

3. ☐ hours, ☐ minutes

4. ☐ hours, ☐ minutes

Save the Date

The Gallagher family doesn't like to have more than one activity scheduled per day. CIRCLE each thing that the family can do from the list of events.

SUNDAY	MONDAY	TUESDAY	WEDNESDAY	THURSDAY	FRIDAY	SATURDAY
			1	2	3	4 Jody's soccer game
5	6	7 Jody's soccer practice	8	9 Becky's dance class	10 Play date with Alex	11
12 Dad's birthday dinner	13	14 Jody's soccer practice	15 Field trip to the zoo	16	17	18
19	20	21 Jody's soccer practice	22	23 Becky's dance class	24	25 Apple picking
26	27	28 Jody's soccer practice	29	30		

SEPTEMBER

Ricky's birthday party, September 25

Dinner with the Hasani family, September 6

Family yoga, September 19

Book club, September 28

Parent-teacher night, September 13

Scout bowling party, September 1

My Birthday Day

Some friends are curious to find out on which day of the week their birthdays will be. WRITE the day of the week for each friend's birthday.

JANUARY
S M T W T F S
1 2 3
4 5 6 7 8 9 10
11 12 13 14 15 16 17
18 19 20 21 22 23 24
25 26 27 28 29 30 31

FEBRUARY
S M T W T F S
1 2 3 4 5 6 7
8 9 10 11 12 13 14
15 16 17 18 19 20 21
22 23 24 25 26 27 28

MARCH
S M T W T F S
1 2 3 4 5 6 7
8 9 10 11 12 13 14
15 16 17 18 19 20 21
22 23 24 25 26 27 28
29 30 31

APRIL
S M T W T F S
1 2 3 4
5 6 7 8 9 10 11
12 13 14 15 16 17 18
19 20 21 22 23 24 25
26 27 28 29 30

MAY
S M T W T F S
1 2
3 4 5 6 7 8 9
10 11 12 13 14 15 16
17 18 19 20 21 22 23
24 25 26 27 28 29 30
31

JUNE
S M T W T F S
1 2 3 4 5 6
7 8 9 10 11 12 13
14 15 16 17 18 19 20
21 22 23 24 25 26 27
28 29 30

JULY
S M T W T F S
1 2 3 4
5 6 7 8 9 10 11
12 13 14 15 16 17 18
19 20 21 22 23 24 25
26 27 28 29 30 31

AUGUST
S M T W T F S
1
2 3 4 5 6 7 8
9 10 11 12 13 14 15
16 17 18 19 20 21 22
23 24 25 26 27 28 29
30 31

SEPTEMBER
S M T W T F S
1 2 3 4 5
6 7 8 9 10 11 12
13 14 15 16 17 18 19
20 21 22 23 24 25 26
27 28 29 30

OCTOBER
S M T W T F S
1 2 3
4 5 6 7 8 9 10
11 12 13 14 15 16 17
18 19 20 21 22 23 24
25 26 27 28 29 30 31

NOVEMBER
S M T W T F S
1 2 3 4 5 6 7
8 9 10 11 12 13 14
15 16 17 18 19 20 21
22 23 24 25 26 27 28
29 30

DECEMBER
S M T W T F S
1 2 3 4 5
6 7 8 9 10 11 12
13 14 15 16 17 18 19
20 21 22 23 24 25 26
27 28 29 30 31

1. June 4 _____

2. February 22 _____

3. May 18 _____

4. November 5 _____

5. March 17 _____

6. January 10 _____

7. October 28 _____

8. August 7 _____

Get Organized

Paul has every date he needs to know written down on lots of small pieces of paper. He bought a calendar to get organized. WRITE all of the information onto the calendar.

April 17
Concert in the park

The first baseball practice is the second Thursday in April.

Earth Day
April 22

American Dance-Off

premieres on TV May 3.

Mother's Day is May 9.

Mom & Dad's anniversary is May 18.

Dentist appointment on May 12.

Don't forget Stella's birthday April 18.

APRIL

Sunday	Monday	Tuesday	Wednesday	Thursday	Friday	Saturday
				1	2	3
4	5	6	7	8	9	10
11	12	13	14	15	16	17
18	19	20	21	22	23	24
25	26	27	28	29	30	

MAY

Sunday	Monday	Tuesday	Wednesday	Thursday	Friday	Saturday
						1
2	3	4	5	6	7	8
9	10	11	12	13	14	15
16	17	18	19	20	21	22
23 / 30	24 / 31	25	26	27	28	29

Chipping In

Three friends are chipping in their money to buy lunch. WRITE the total amount of money the friends have.

Total $ [ ] . [ ]

Short Changed

Each register shows the change the person should receive, and the change is on the counter. CIRCLE any picture that does **not** have the correct change.

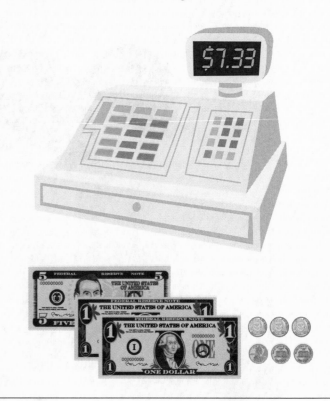

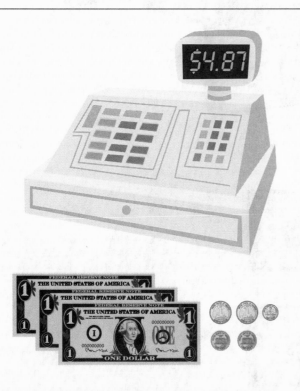

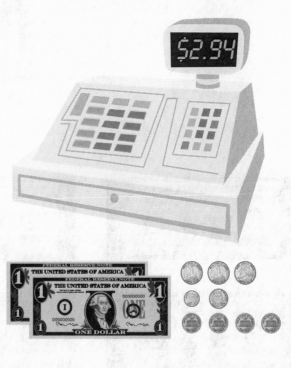

Money Values

Saving Up

Sonya is saving up to buy a $10.00 book. She has $7.58 saved already. CIRCLE the money that she still needs to make $10.00.

What's in the Wallet?

WRITE the total amount of money each person has.

1. Anthony has 1 five-dollar bill, 2 one-dollar bills,
   3 dimes, and 1 nickel in his wallet. $_____

2. Skylar has 4 one-dollar bills, 3 quarters,
   2 dimes, and 4 pennies in her wallet. $_____

3. Devon has 2 five-dollar bills, 1 one-dollar bill,
   2 quarters, 3 nickels, and 8 pennies in his wallet. $_____

4. Abby has 1 five-dollar bill, 3 one-dollar bills, 5 quarters,
   4 dimes, 2 nickels, and 2 pennies in her wallet. $_____

5. Jonah has 3 one-dollar bills, 6 quarters, 3 dimes,
   4 nickels, and 3 pennies in his wallet. $_____

6. Naomi has 1 five-dollar bill, 4 one-dollar bills, 1 quarter,
   7 dimes, 5 nickels, and 9 pennies in her wallet. $_____

Vending Machine

CIRCLE each thing you could afford to buy in the vending machine.

Pay the Check

CIRCLE the money needed to pay the check using exact change.

GUEST CHECK	
Date	Table	Guests	Server	**100044**

Cheeseburger	$ 8.73
French fries	$ 1.95
Lemonade	$ 2.26
Ice cream sundae	$ 5.44
Total	$18.38

Pick a Present

Mickey would like to buy a present for a girl he likes, and he wants to buy the most expensive thing he can buy with the money he has. CIRCLE the present Mickey should buy.

$15.43

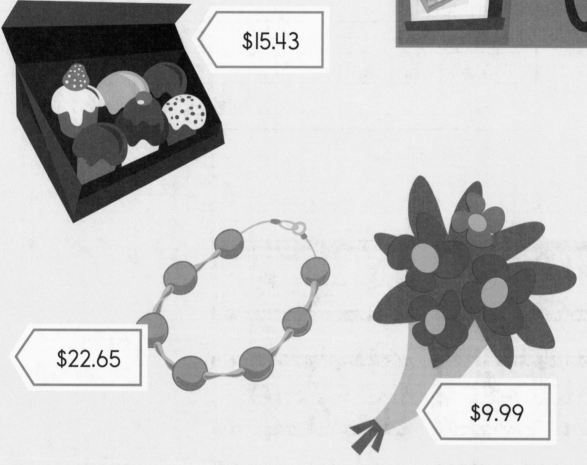

$22.65

$9.99

Once Upon a Time

The Beast was trying to look good for Beauty, so he went to the salon. WRITE the total cost of the Beast's day at the salon.

Claw cleaning	$12.85
Mane grooming	$ 9.66
Fur conditioning	$ 5.03
Fang buffing	$ 6.40

Total cost $ ___ . ___

Paper Route

Four friends each deliver newspapers. They were curious to find out who made the most money in a week. CIRCLE the hand of the friend who made the most money.

Going Green

Four people have cut down on their electricity use and have saved money on their electric bills. Each person is holding the amount of money that was saved since last month's bill. CIRCLE the hand of the person that saved the most.

⚡Electric Company

June total $72.44

July total $69.28

⚡Electric Company

June total $80.04

July total $72.96

⚡Electric Company

June total $74.25

July total $68.27

⚡Electric Company

June total $82.16

July total $74.89

Vending Machine

WRITE the numbers 1 through 9 so that 1 is the most expensive item and 9 is the least expensive item.

Best Price

It's always good to shop around for low prices. CIRCLE the item in each row that has the lowest price.

$10.58

$10.75

$11.02

$12.35

$11.99

$13.41

$19.99

$20.05

$19.79

$35.55

$34.98

$35.19

Picture Graphs

Wet Weather

In this graph, one picture is equal to the weather for one day in the month of April. LOOK at the graph, and ANSWER the questions.

April Weather

Sunny	☀ ☀ ☀ ☀ ☀ ☀ ☀ ☀ ☀ ☀
Cloudy	⛅ ⛅ ⛅ ⛅ ⛅
Rainy	🌧 🌧 🌧 🌧 🌧 🌧 🌧 🌧 🌧
Stormy	⛈ ⛈ ⛈ ⛈ ⛈ ⛈

1. How many days were rainy in April? _____

2. How many days were sunny? _____

3. How many days were either rainy or stormy? _____

4. What kind of weather did April have for the most number of days? _____

5. How many more days were sunny than stormy? _____

6. How many more days were rainy than cloudy? _____

Bestseller Books

In this graph, one book cover is equal to 10 books sold. LOOK at the graph, and ANSWER the questions.

 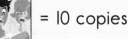 = 10 copies

Number of Books Sold

Erased	(8 covers)
Zombie Pirates!	(9 covers)
Mickey Comes Home	(6 covers)
Amazing Rescue!	(11 covers)
Torn Apart	(7 covers)

1. How many copies of *Mickey Comes Home* were sold? _____

2. How many copies of *Zombie Pirates!* were sold? _____

3. What was the bestselling book? _____

4. What was the worst selling book? _____

5. Which book sold 10 more copies than *Erased*?

_____

6. Which book sold 30 fewer copies than *Amazing Rescue!*?

_____

Picture Graphs

Graph It

Use this page to collect data to complete the graph on the opposite page. ASK 15 people what kind of pet they have: a dog, a cat, a fish, a rabbit, a bird, a different kind of pet, or no pet. WRITE their answers. If people have more than one pet, write down each kind of pet. Then DRAW the pets to complete the graph.

Name: _____   Type of pet: _____

Name: _____   Type of pet: _____

Name: _____   Type of pet: _____

Name: _____   Type of pet: _____

Name: _____   Type of pet: _____

Name: _____   Type of pet: _____

Name: _____   Type of pet: _____

Name: _____   Type of pet: _____

Name: _____   Type of pet: _____

Name: _____   Type of pet: _____

Name: _____   Type of pet: _____

Name: _____   Type of pet: _____

Name: _____   Type of pet: _____

Name: _____   Type of pet: _____

Name: _____   Type of pet: _____

Pet Popularity

Dog	
Cat	
Fish	
Rabbit	
Bird	
Other O	
None N	

Yummy Vegetables

Penelope asked everyone she knew to name their favorite vegetable, and then she graphed the results. LOOK at the graph, and ANSWER the questions.

Favorite Vegetables

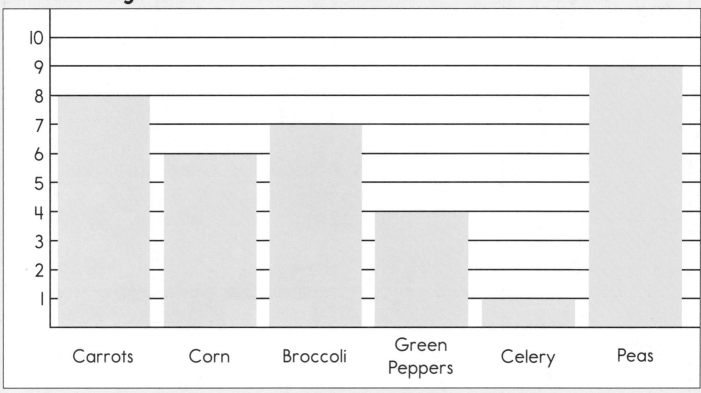

1. Which vegetable did six people choose as their favorite? _____

2. How many people like broccoli best? _____

3. How many people chose either peas or carrots? _____

4. How many more people like corn than celery? _____

5. What is the most popular choice for a favorite vegetable?

   _____

6. How many people did Penelope ask about their favorite vegetable?

   _____

Push It Up!

A school has just started a new fitness program and checked how many push-ups each student could do at the start of the program. LOOK at the graph, and ANSWER the questions.

Push-ups at the Beginner Level

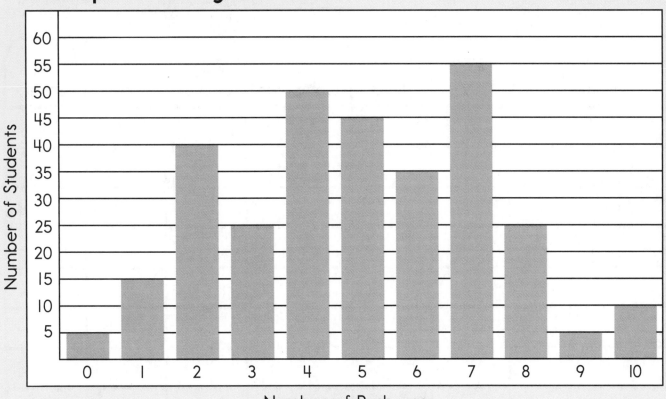

Number of Push-ups

1. How many students did six push-ups? _____

2. How many students did three push-ups? _____

3. How many students couldn't do any push-ups? _____

4. What was the number of push-ups that the most students could do?

_____

5. How many students could do eight or more push-ups? _____

6. How many students could do fewer than three push-ups? _____

Graph It

Use this page to collect data to complete the graph on the opposite page. ASK 15 people about their favorite way to spend their free time. Ask if they prefer to watch TV, read, spend time on the computer, play video games, play sports, or something else. RECORD their answers. Then DRAW the graph.

Name	Watch TV	Read	Computer	Video Games	Sports	Other

Favorite Way to Spend Time

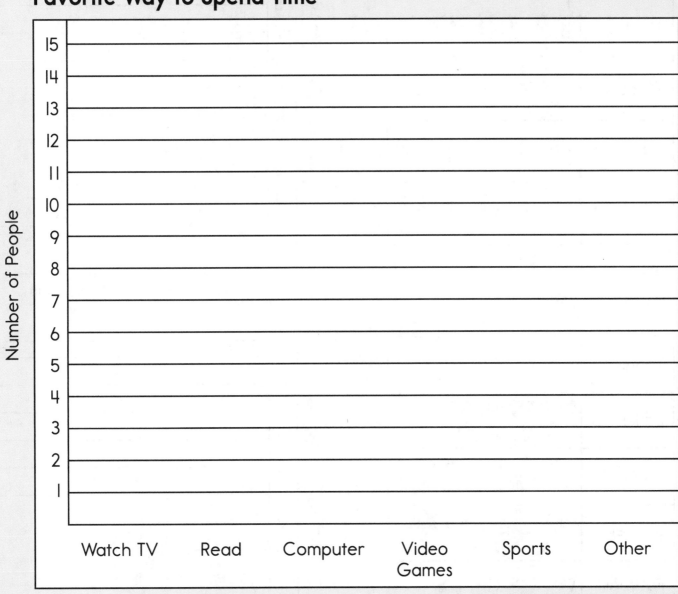

Number of People

| 15 |
| 14 |
| 13 |
| 12 |
| 11 |
| 10 |
| 9 |
| 8 |
| 7 |
| 6 |
| 5 |
| 4 |
| 3 |
| 2 |
| 1 |

Watch TV　　Read　　Computer　　Video Games　　Sports　　Other

Favorite Activities

Graph Grabber

CIRCLE the graph that works best with the title "People's Favorite Sports."

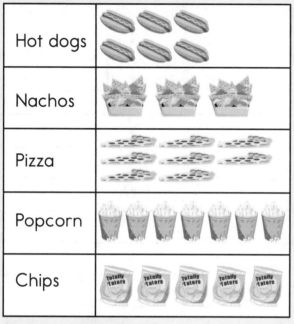

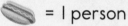 = 1 person

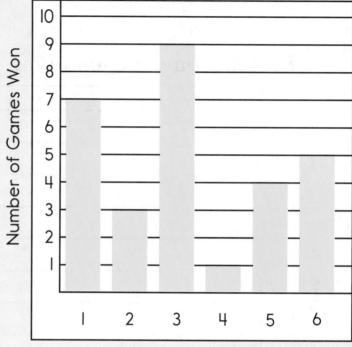

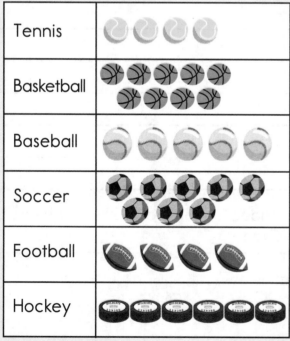

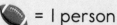 = 1 person

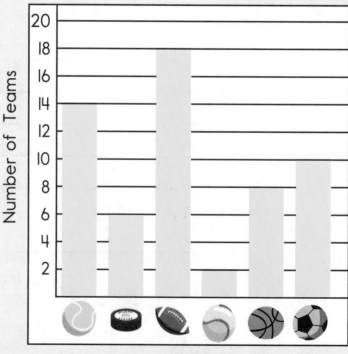

Answers

Page 210

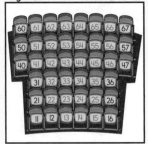

Page 211

Page 212

Page 213

BJI 546	ARR 767	928 SQF
BJI 547	ARR 768	929 SQF
BJI 548	ARR 769	930 SQF
BJI 549	ARR 770	931 SQF
BJI 550	ARR 771	932 SQF
BJI 551	ARR 772	933 SQF
BJI 552	ARR 773	934 SQF

Page 214

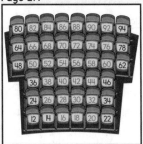

Page 215

1. 8	2. 16	3. 24
4. 32	5. 40	6. 48
7. 56	8. 64	9. 72

Page 216

Electric Company — Martinez Family — Billing Month: January — Amount Due: $76

Electric Company — Martinez Family — Billing Month: December — Amount Due: $113

Electric Company — Martinez Family — Billing Month: May — Amount Due: $79

Electric Company — Martinez Family — Billing Month: August — Amount Due: $132

Page 217

1. MIA 806	2. JIN 799
3. MAX 736	4. KEN 645
5. AMY 568	6. DAN 421
7. TED 310	8. SAM 279

Page 218

1. Willis Tower
2. Petronas Towers
3. Petronas Towers
4. Jin Mao Tower
5. Willis Tower
6. Empire State Building
7. Petronas Towers
8. Jin Mao Tower

Page 219

312 — 6, 368 — 2, 321 — 5, 355 — 3, 339 — 4, 382 — 1

Page 220

1. 30	2. 40	3. 60
4. 10	5. 100	6. 80
7. 80	8. 70	9. 20
10. 90	11. 40	12. 50

Page 221

1. 500	2. 400	3. 300
4. 800	5. 200	6. 600
7. 400	8. 700	9. 800
10. 100		

Page 222

Check: 63

Page 223

Check: 84

Page 224

1. 25	2. 38
3. 69	4. 77

Page 225

42	48	43	36	50	32
37	40	54	43	44	27
79	88	97	79	94	59

Page 226

1. 68	2. 78
3. 79	4. 58

Page 227

1. 34	2. 70	3. 16
4. 23	5. 45	6. 2

Page 228

1. 90	2. 72	3. 25
4. 44	5. 76	

Page 229

$72 — Buy It Now! — $12 OFF

Page 230

1. 81	2. 53	3. 84
4. 73	5. 44	6. 90
7. 78		

Page 231

71

Page 232

1. 111	2. 138

Page 233

1. 33	2. 44
3. 68	4. 80

Page 234

1. 45	2. 28	3. 48
4. 29	5. 37	6. 19
7. 65	8. 38	

Page 235

1. 86	2. 19	3. 13
4. 27	5. 76	

Page 236

$61 — ANN'S ATHLETIC SUPPLY $25 OFF

Page 237

64 − 15 = 49
34 − 29 = 6
41 − 27 = 16
93 − 58 = 35
82 − 34 = 46
56 − 19 = 37
66 − 58 = 8
75 − 46 = 39
95 − 18 = 77
33 − 9 = 25
45 − 17 = 28
81 − 23 = 68

Page 238

5

Page 239

8

Page 240

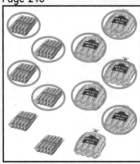

Page 241

6

Page 242

8

Page 243

6

Page 244

12

Page 245

5

Page 246

Page 247

Answers

Page 248

Page 249

Page 250

Page 251

Suggestion:

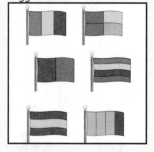

Page 252

Page 253

1. $\frac{1}{2}$ 2. $\frac{1}{4}$ 3. $\frac{2}{3}$
4. $\frac{3}{4}$ 5. $\frac{1}{3}$

Page 254

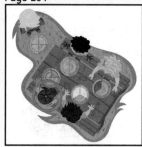

Page 255

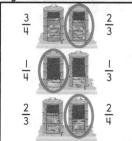

$\frac{3}{4}$ $\frac{2}{3}$
$\frac{1}{4}$ $\frac{1}{3}$
$\frac{2}{3}$ $\frac{2}{4}$

Page 256

1. 2   2. 1   3. 3
4. 3   5. 1   6. 2

Page 257

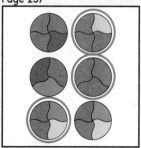

Page 258

Page 259

1. 1   2. 1
3. 2   4. 4

Page 260

Page 261

1. 7   2. 4
3. 5   4. 6

Page 262

Page 263

Have someone check your answers.

Page 264

1. Leaf insect
2. Hissing cockroach
3. Praying mantis
4. Katydid

Page 265

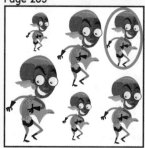

Page 266

Have someone check your answers.

Page 267

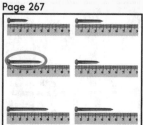

Page 268

1. 6   2. 10   3. 3
4. 7   5. 11

Page 269

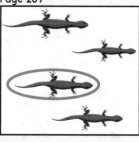

Page 270

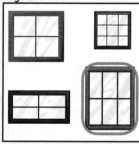

Page 271

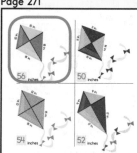

Page 272

52

Page 273

Suggestion:

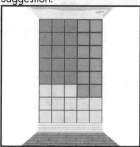

Page 274

308

Answers

Page 275

1.
(drawings of items 1-4)

Page 276

Page 277

1. 2. 3. 4.

Page 278
1. 3:00
2. 1:30
3. 7:15
4. 12:30
5. 11:30
6. 1:45

Page 279
1. 1, 30
2. 1, 45
3. 4, 15
4. 0, 45

Page 280
1. 5, 0
2. 3, 30
3. 2, 45
4. 1, 15

Page 281
1. 3, 30
2. 4, 45
3. 7, 15
4. 2, 30

Page 282
Dinner with the Hasani family, September 6
Family yoga, September 19
Parent-teacher night, September 13
Scout bowling party, September 1

Page 283
1. Thursday
2. Sunday
3. Monday
4. Thursday
5. Tuesday
6. Saturday
7. Wednesday
8. Friday

Pages 284–285

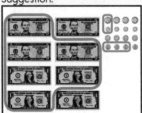

Page 286
16.51

Page 287

Page 288
Suggestion:

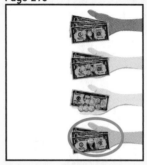

Page 289
1. 7.35
2. 4.99
3. 11.73
4. 9.77
5. 5.03
6. 10.29

Page 290

Page 291
Suggestion:

Page 292

Page 293
33.94

Page 294

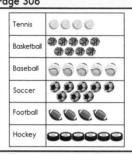

Page 295

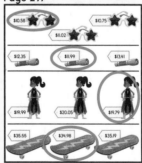

Page 296

Page 297

Page 298
1. 9
2. 10
3. 15
4 sunny
5. 4
6. 4

Page 299
1. 60
2. 90
3. Amazing Rescue!
4. Mickey Comes Home
5. Zombie Pirates!
6. Erased

Pages 300–301
Have someone check your answers.

Page 302
1. corn
2. 7
3. 17
4. 5
5. peas
6. 35

Page 303
1. 35
2. 25
3. 5
4. 7
5. 40
6. 60

Pages 304–305
Have someone check your answers.

Page 306

Tennis					
Basketball					
Baseball					
Soccer					
Football					
Hockey					